The Good Citizen

★　　★　　★　　★

The Good Citizen

★ ★ ★ ★

edited by

David Batstone and Eduardo Mendieta

Routledge
New York   London

Published in 1999 by
Routledge
29 West 35th Street
New York, NY 10001

Published in Great Britain by
Routledge
11 New Fetter Lane
London EC4P 4EE

10 9 8 7 6 5 4 3 2 1

Library of Congress Cataloging-in-Publication Data

The good citizen / edited by David Batstone and Eduardo Mendieta.
        p. cm.
     Includes bibliographical references.
     ISBN 0-415-92093-0
     1. Civics. 2. Citizenship—United States. 3. Political participation—United
States. I. Batstone, David B., 1958–   . II. Mendieta, Eduardo.
JK1759.G58 1998
323.6'0973—dc21   98-37926
                                                                        CIP

David: To Wendy,
who emigrated from Down Under, and our children, dual citizens,
whose second language is Spanglish.

Eduardo: To Jenny,
who married an immigrant, and our children,
whose first language is Spanglish.

Contents

★   ★   ★

What Does it Mean to be an American?

★   ★   ★

David Batstone and Eduardo Mendieta

Consider the image on the front of this book. A flag, an American flag, or rather *the* flag. Yet the flag on the cover of the book isn't a flag at all. It's a painting of the flag of the United States of America entitled *Flag* by Jasper Johns. We selected this image — ironic and self-reflexive — to underscore the perils and paradoxes of any kind of representation. The American flag is a symbol so laden with meaning that the art critic Robert Hughes has described it as "a kind of eucharistic symbol." Sacred, then, in some way. Many politicians have urged a Constitutional amendment that would make it a crime to desecrate, mangle, violate, burn, or otherwise misuse it. And yet, as Hughes points out, "Americans make jeans, t-shirts, and underwear out of it, and use it to advertise everything from gas stations to hot-dog stands."

A flag, after all, doesn't mean anything by itself. It's an empty signifier, however powerful it may become. The flag is often used to evoke patriotism, and it can call up sincere tears of gratitude and reverence. But it can be used for the most pedestrian, even vulgar, displays of commercialism. The flag is a symbol of our covenant with one another, but it can easily be an alibi for our entrepreneurial spirit, a vehicle for the celebration of what the philosopher Jürgen Habermas has called our "chauvinism of affluence." Sometimes our flag is used to mean that consumption and commodification are our only viable forms of patriotism and citizenship, conveying the simple message that "to be American" is "to buy American."

The flag "means" all these things because its power — its meaning — derives from its symbolic use by a given community over time. We might, then, think of a flag not as an object but as a history — the history of the acts of representation undertaken by a community of citizens.

Like the representation of the flag on the cover of this book, the word "good" in the title is ambiguous, and fraught with resonance. "The good" is ethereal and abstract, but "the goods" are material, specific, and concrete. In America, if you've got the goods, you can deliver. Our book argues, among other things, that a good citizen is one who has the goods, the wherewithal to live out her or his role as a social agent. Or to put it another way, the "good" citizen is one who enjoys the material conditions for the performance of their citizenship. At the same time, the "good" citizen is also one who makes a life commitment to maintaining and sharing with other fellow citizens those material conditions that enable political participation. In short, the "good citizen" underscores the realization that citizenship is a matter of both institutions and values, material interests and ideals.

Some may rightly object that the term "good" is too porous, too open to misunderstanding. But our alternatives struck us as misleading, or too quick to bring closure. We thought of the global citizen, the American citizen, the multicultural citizen, the virtuous citizen, the moral citizen, the postnational citizen, the patriotic citizen. But for us, "good" holds all these concepts within itself.

This is a book of essays reflecting, together, on a problem with no simple solution. It is, in fact, a problem that embraces everyone within the borders of the United States — from the billionaire investor to the illegal immigrant working as a chambermaid in a bordertown motel, a problem as old as Plato and as current as tomorrow's papers. And as that life history would suggest, it's not a problem that we can simply "solve" or that will, on its own, be resolved and disappear. The problem involves the politics of left and right, the ethics of rich and poor, the internationalization of corporations, the idea of national boundaries in a global society. It involves notions of groups and classes and bodies politic. In a nutshell, we ask here: How can we be good *and* be citizens of the United States? This isn't necessarily a question of morality or ethics, though for some it will in part be that. But in asking "What would the good citizen be?" we're asking a lot more. Is citizenship something susceptible to improvement, so that someone might become *good at* being an American? Is the good citizen, like the good Samaritan, an anomalous figure of virtue, invoked with respect on last night's local news? Civic saints, like the other kind, have always been scarce.

Like the citizens it describes and addresses, this is a book united by place, history, and a common set of concerns. Its subject is citizenship, considered as an ideal and a practical identity, and embracing of both moral value and pragmatic institution. As a moral and ideal pursuit, it demands that we engage in a deliberation about the values that give direction to our political community. Michael Lerner notes that while the Right has been able to manipulate the discourses of morality, but remains silent about economics, the Left has focused its attention merely on economic and political issues, while ignoring the importance of meaning, values, and community. Part of citizenship is acknowledging the moral responsibility it entails.

As an ideal, citizenship stands for the autonomy, self-legislation, and sense of civic solidarity that members of a group extend to one another. Through citizenship we affirm our autonomy on the one hand, while on the other dictating the obligations that constrain our expression of that autonomy. Through citizenship we are both subjects and objects of the law. At the same time, it is through citizenship that we are commanded to stand in solidarity with others in our community. Citizenship secularizes the commandment to treat the stranger as one's neighbor. Citizenship makes friends of enemies, compatriots of anonymous others. Walt Whitman argues that without gentleness and spiritual union this country would be among the fabled damned of nations. "Affection between citizens," he counseled, is "necessary for democracy to work."

The essays in this book represent nine thinkers, in their own voices, on aspects of citizenship. Cornel West asks us to engage not only our political and civic obligations, but our moral ones as well, and to resist any artificial separation of the civic from the moral. Robert N. Bellah considers the extent and consequences of polarization in today's world. David Batstone asks us to reconceive our commitment to personal justice and freedom in a world irreversibly altered by technology. Barbara Christian helps us wonder at, and understand, ideas of innocence in a world as complex as our own. Michael Lerner asks how we have come to see "values" as the property of the Right, and why the concept seems to be invisible on the Left. Ronald Takaki explores another kind of invisibility, that of the non-white American. Linda Martín Alcoff and Eduardo Mendieta examine Hispanic identity politics and what it tells us about becoming — not merely being — a citizen. Judith Butler shows that the controversy over gays in the military is central to any theory of citizenship in America.

Like any book about citizenship, this is a book partly about politics. We don't expect it to transcend political distinctions, but we think its issues challenge readers on both imaginary ends of the political spectrum, as well as everyone in the middle. "The good citizen" may be an ideal, but it's an ideal won through tough thinking on practical matters. These essays challenge us to think hard about what we mean when we call ourselves Americans. But most of all it is about the individual, the dependent, independent individual, always and never alone in the modern world.

ONE

The Moral Obligations of Living in a Democratic Society

★   ★   ★

Cornel West

One of the fundamental questions of our day is whether the tradition of struggle can be preserved and expanded. I refer to the struggle for decency and dignity, the struggle for freedom and democracy.

In *Tradition and Individual Talent* (1919), T. S. Eliot claims that tradition is not something you inherit — if you want it, you must sacrifice for it. In other words, tradition must be fought for.

We live at the end of a century of unprecedented brutality and barbarity, a period when more than two hundred million fellow human beings have been murdered in the name of some pernicious ideology. Nazism was at the heart of a so-called civilized Europe. Stalinism was at the core of a so-called emancipatory Soviet Union. European colonialism and imperialism in Africa, South America, and Asia have left palpable and lasting scars on fellow human beings. Patriarchal subordination of sisters of all colors and all regions and all countries is evident. The devaluation and degradation of gay brothers and lesbian sisters across race, region, and class, as well as the marginalization of the disabled and physically challenged.

What kind of species are we? What leads us to think that the tradition of struggle for decency and dignity can be preserved into the twenty-first century? Or will it be the case that we shall witness in the twenty-first century the unleashing of new, unnameable and indescribable forms of agony and anguish? At the moment, we are right to fear the emergence of ancient tribalisms that are revitalized under the aegis of an uncontested global capitalism, a movement accompanied by the "gangsterization" of community, nation, and the globe.

What attracts me to the Black-Jewish dialogue is the potential that is inherent to our respective traditions of struggle. It has nothing to do with skin pigmentation *per se*, nor with ethnicity in the abstract. Rather, it is because these two communities have developed a set of responses to combat the fundamental problem of evil.

The problem of evil refers to working out a response to undeserved suffering, unmerited pain, and unjustified harm. It is impossible to talk about Jews or Blacks, symbolically or literally, without discussing the problem of evil because these groups have been consistently devalued and subjugated, if not downright hated and despised. Indeed, the history of that treatment raises very alien dilemmas for America.

Henry James was correct when he declared America to be a "hotel civilization." In fact, this is the reason James left the country; he experienced American society as being too bland and culturally impoverished. At the turn of the twentieth century, America did not want to deal with the problem of evil, let alone the tragic and the comic — it was too preoccupied with the melodramatic and the sentimental.

A hotel — the fusion of a home and a market — is such a wonderful metaphor for America. The warmth, security, and motherhood of the home exists, as does that patriarchal tilt that burdens sisters of all colors, to caretake men who must forage in the marketplace. The men go forth into a heartless world, in a quest for mobility, liquidity, and profit-making. This fusion of home and market has its own distinct ethos: privatistic, individualistic, tribalistic, ethnic-centered, racially subscribed, distrustful of the nation-state, distrustful of bureaucracy, and marginalizing of public interest and the common good.

It is no coincidence then, that the best of the Jewish and Black traditions has consistently infused a sense of the tragic and the comic in order to expand the precious traditions of their struggle. In my own case, I began to struggle with the problem of evil by grappling with the absurd, the absurd in America and the absurd *as* America. I did not have to read a book by Jean-Paul Sartre or see a play by Samuel Beckett to understand what the absurd was. I had a black body in a civilization deeply shaped by white supremacist perceptions, sensibilities, and institutional practices. When something as irrational and arbitrary as skin pigmentation is the benchmark of measuring one's humanity, then that state of affairs is totally absurd.

What is distinctive about this precious experiment in democracy called America is that it has always been inextricably interwoven with white supremacy and its legacy. Although some scholars call it an irony, I call it a hypocrisy. John J. Chapman described it accurately when he concluded that white supremacy was like a serpent wrapped around the legs of the table upon which the Declaration of Independence was signed by the founding fathers. It haunted America then and nearly 220 years later it still does. The challenge for America today is whether it will continue to deny, evade, and avoid various forms of evil in its midst.

In any discussion about race matters it is vital to situate yourself in a tradition, in a larger narrative that links the past to the present. When we think of Sojourner Truth, Harriet Tubman, Ida Buelle, Wells Barnett, A. Philip Randolph, Marcus Garvey, Ella Baker, James Baldwin, and so many nameless and anonymous ones, we cannot but be moved by their standards of vision and courage. They are wind at one's back.

The recovery of a tradition always begins at the existential level, with the experience of what it is to be human under a specific set of circumstances and conditions. It is very difficult to engage in a candid and frank critical discussion about race by assuming it is going to be a rational exchange. Race must be addressed in a form that can deal with its complexity and irrationality.

Perhaps no one understood the existential dimension of being human and African in America better than W. E. B. Du Bois. He recognized the absurd in American society and realized that being Black in America is to be a problem. Du Bois asserted that race in this country is the fetishization of a problem, black bodies in white space. He understood what it meant to be cast as part of a problem people rather than people with problems. Once the humanity of a people is problematized, they are called into question perennially. Their beauty is attacked:

wrong hips, lips, noses, skin texture, skin pigmentation, and hair texture. Black intelligence is always guilty before proven innocent in the
court of the life of the mind; *The Bell Curve* is just a manifestation of
the cycle. Perhaps the gravest injustice is the image of the welfare
queen. Looking at the history of black women in America, on the plantation taking care of white children in white households, how is it possible that they could become the symbol of laziness? All of the
foregoing are signs of a humanity that has been problematized.

Du Bois also underscored that to be part of a problem people is to
be viewed as part of an undifferentiated blob, a monolithic block.
Problem people become indistinguishable and interchangeable, which
means that only one of them has to be asked to find out what all the
rest of them think.

It is rare in human history, of course, that the notion of individuality and the civic are coupled so that a democratic project is generated.
For most of history ordinary people have been viewed as "weeds and
rain drops," as part of a mob, a rabble, all of which are ways of constituting them as an undifferentiated mob. Even the Greeks, despite their
glorious yet truncated democratic experiment, would only apply the
tragic to the elite. Ordinary people were limited to the idyllic and the
comic, the assumption being that their lives were less complex and
one-dimensional.

A democratic sensibility undeniably cuts against the grain of history. Most of human history is the history of elites, of kings, queens,
princes, prelates, magistrates, potentates, knights, earls, and squires,
all of whom subordinated and exploited everyday people.

This is why it becomes vital to talk about prevailing forms of oligarchy and plutocracy, and to some degree "pigmentocracy," in America. One percent of the population owns 48 percent of the total net
financial wealth. The top 10 percent owns 86 percent of the wealth,
while the top 20 percent owns 94 percent of the wealth. Meanwhile,
80 percent of the our population is experiencing stagnating and declining wages.

Corporations speak glibly about downsizing — bureaucratic language that simply means you do not have a job even though we have
the highest profits we have had since 1948. And yet 25 percent of all

of America's children live in poverty, and 42 percent of young brown brothers and sisters live in poverty, and 51 percent of young black brothers and sisters live in poverty in the richest nation in the history of the world. These sets of conditions are immoral.

When I examine the present state of American democracy, I believe we are living in one of the most terrifying moments in the history of this nation. We are experiencing a lethal and unprecedented linkage of relative economic decline (i.e., working class wage stagnation), cultural decay, and political lethargy. No democracy can survive with a middle class so insecure that it is willing to accept any authoritarian option in order to provide some sense of normalcy and security in their lives. It also opens the door for significant segments of that middle class to scapegoat those who are most vulnerable.

It is past time that we consider in our public discourse the civic responsibilities of corporations. There must be prescribed forms of public accountability for institutions that have a disproportionate amount of wealth, power, and influence. This is not a matter of demonizing corporations, but an issue of democratic survival.

We are all in the same boat, on the same turbulent sea. The boat has a huge leak in it and in the end, we go up and down together. A corporate executive recently said to me, "We are not in the same boat. We're global." His response suggests why it is vital to inquire when corporate commercial interests must be subordinate to the public interest.

Democracy always raises the fundamental question: What is the role of the most disadvantaged in relation to the public interest? It is similar in some ways to the biblical question: What are you to do with the least of these? If we do not want to live in a democracy, we are not obliged to raise that question. In fact, the aristocracy does not address that question at all. Chekhov wrote in a play, "The Czar's police, they don't give a damn about raising that question. That's not the kind of society they are." But within a democratic society that question must be continually raised and pushed.

The conversation matters because the preservation of democracy is threatened by real economic decline. While it is not identical to moral and cultural decay, it is inseparable from it. Even though the pocketbook is important, many Americans are concerned more about the low quality of their lives, the constant fear of violent assault and cruel insult, the mean spiritedness and cold heartedness of social life, and the inability to experience deep levels of intimacy. These are the signs of a culturally decadent civilization.

By "decadent" I mean the relative erosion of systems of nurturing and caring, which affects each of us, but which has an especially devastating impact on young people. Any civilization that is unable to sustain its networks of caring and nurturing will generate enough anger and aggression to make communication near impossible. The result is a society in which we do not even respect each other enough to listen to each other. Dialogue is the lifeblood of democracy and is predicated on certain bonds of trust and respect. At this moment of cultural decay, it is difficult to find places where those ties of sympathy may be nurtured.

The roots of democracy are fundamentally grounded in mutual respect, personal responsibility, and social accountability. Yet democracy is also about giving each person a dignified voice in the decision-making processes in those institutions that guide and regulate their lives. These deeply moral suppositions have a certain spiritual dimension. John Dewey and Josiah Royce, among others, identified a spirituality of genuine questioning and dialogical exchange that allows us to transcend our egocentric predicaments. Spirituality requires an experience of something bigger than our individual selves that binds us to a community. It could be in an authoritarian bind, of course, which is why the kind of spiritual and moral awakening that is necessary for a democracy to function is based on a sense of the public — a sense of what it is to be a citizen among citizens.

Nurturing spirituality is so difficult today because we are bombarded by a market culture that evolves around buying and selling, promoting and advertising. The market tries to convince us that we are really alive only when we are addicted to stimulation and titillation. Given the fact that so much of American culture revolves around sexual foreplay and orgiastic intensity, for many people the good life might mean being hooked up to an orgasm machine and being perennially titillated.

The ultimate logic of a market culture is the gangsterization of culture: I want power now. I want pleasure now. I want property now. Your property. Give it to me.

Young black people call their block a "hood" now. I grew up in a neighborhood; it is a big difference. A neighborhood was a place not only for the nuclear family, but also included aunts and uncles, friends and neighbors, rabbis and priests, deacons and pastors, Little League coaches and dance teachers — all of whom served as a backdrop for socializing young people. This backdrop provided children with a sense of what it is to be human, with all its decency, integrity, and compassion. When those values are practiced, a neighborhood emerges.

Unfortunately, neighborhoods often took shape in my boyhood under patriarchal and homophobic conditions, and that history must be called into question. Still, we must recover its flow of nonmarket values and nonmarket activity.

These days we cannot even talk about love the way James Baldwin and Martin Luther King Jr. did. Nobody wants to hear that syrupy, mushy stuff. James Baldwin, however, said love is the most dangerous discourse in the world. It is daring and difficult because it makes you vulnerable, but if you experience it, it is the peak of human existence.

In our own time it is becoming extremely difficult for nonmarket values to gain a foothold. Parenting is a nonmarket activity; so much sacrifice and service goes into it without any assurance that the providers will get anything back. Mercy, justice; they are nonmarket. Care, service; nonmarket. Solidarity, fidelity; nonmarket. Sweetness and kindness and gentleness. All nonmarket.

Tragically, nonmarket values are relatively scarce, which is one of the reasons why it is so tough to mobilize and organize people in our society around just about any cause. It is hard to convince people that there are alternative options for which they ought to sacrifice. Ultimately, there can be no democratic tradition without nonmarket values.

In the last decade we have witnessed within popular culture wonderful innovation in forms of hip hop and rap. Compare that phenomenon to the 1960s when the Black Panther Party emerged and note the big difference between the two movements. One has to do with sacrifice, paying the price, dealing with the consequences as you bring power and pressure to bear on the prevailing status quo. The other has to do with marketing black rage. One movement had forty-seven local branches across the nation, the other sells millions of albums and CDs. The comparison is not a matter of patronizing this generation. Frankly, it is a critique of each us who has to deal with this market culture and through market mechanisms try to preserve some nonmarket values.

What then are we to do? There is no overnight solution or panacea, of course. We need to begin with something profoundly un-American, namely, recalling a sense of history, a very deep, tragic, and comic sense of history, a historical sensibility linked to empathy. Empathy is not simply a matter of trying to imagine what others are going through, but having the will to muster enough courage to do something about it. In a way, empathy is predicated upon hope.

Hope has nothing to do with optimism. I am in no way optimistic about America, nor am I optimistic about the plight of the human species on this globe. There is simply not enough evidence that allows me to infer that things are going to get better. That has been the perennial state and condition of not simply black people in America, but all self-conscious human beings who are sensitive to the forms of evil around them. We can be prisoners of hope even as we call optimism into question.

To be part of the democratic tradition is to be a prisoner of hope. And you cannot be a prisoner of hope without engaging in a form of struggle in the present moment that keeps the best of the past alive. To engage in that struggle means that one is always willing to acknowledge that there is no triumph around the corner, but that you persist because you believe it is right and just and moral. As T. S. Eliot said, "Ours is in the trying. The rest is not our business."

We are not going to save each other, ourselves, America, or the world. But we certainly can leave it a little bit better. As my grandmother used to say, "If the Kingdom of God is within you, then everywhere you go, you ought to leave a little Heaven behind."

TWO

The Ethics of Polarization in the United States and the World

★ ★ ★

Robert N. Bellah

In thinking about the sweeping changes that are occurring in global and American society, and the implications of those changes for the future, I am afraid that we must face a great deal of very bad news. Since the end of the Cold War, what little seemed to be holding us together is coming apart at the seams. Among the many differences and cleavages that seem to be driving us apart in the world today, the most pernicious are class differences, indeed the massive polarization of social classes in our country and in the world. It is much more common today to focus on racial differences, cultural differences, ethnic differences, and religious differences. Though real enough, all that serves in part as a smokescreen to divert attention from the most profound difference opening up in our world, the difference between the winners and the losers, the rich and the poor.

There is a strange resonance between the last years of the nineteenth century and the last years of our own. In the late nineteenth century capitalist development was in full swing, but it was a development so grossly exploitative, so unequal in its rewards, so patently unfair, that it stimulated the massive opposition of labor unions and socialist parties, which challenged the control of the capitalist class through much of the twentieth century. Now for the first time in one hundred years capitalism has no effective opposition. Not only is

Communism dead and socialism discredited but labor unions are everywhere in shambles. Not only is the difference between the rich and the poor growing rapidly in most of the world (nowhere quite so rapidly as in the United States), but the difference between rich nations and poor nations is also growing apace. During the Cold War the poor nations had some leverage: They were courted by both sides in the global struggle for strategic advantage. With the Cold War over they can simply be abandoned. In some ways the situation is even worse today than it was one hundred years ago.

When someone emphasizes class disparities today he will be accused by conservative ideologists of preaching class war, as I have been. There is a class war today, but it is neither being waged by people like me nor by the people suffering most in today's world. Class war today is being waged ruthlessly, largely effectively, and with little resistance, by the rich on the poor both nationally and globally. Let me be more specific.

It is the global market that is literally tearing the world apart. The forces of the global market economy are impinging on all societies in the world with increasing pressure and the capacity of nation-states to protect their own populations from these pressures — one of the primary functions of the nation-state since the nineteenth century — is everywhere weakening. That means that all of us are subject to similar pressures with similar disconcerting results. I take the chief consequence of these pressures to be the growing disparity between winners and losers in the global marketplace. The result is not only income polarization, with the rich growing richer and the poor poorer, but a shrinking middle class increasingly anxious about its future.

Let us consider some of the tendencies these global pressures are creating everywhere, but with particular sharpness in the United States. First is the emergence of a deracinated elite composed of those Robert Reich calls "symbolic analysts," that is, the people who know how to use the new technologies and information systems that are transforming the global economy. Such people are located less securely in communities than in networks that may link them, flexibly and transiently, to others all over the world. Educated in the highly competitive atmosphere of excellent universities and graduate schools, such persons have learned to travel light with regard to family, church, locality, even nation. It is here, though not exclusively here, that we clearly see the cultural profile of individualization that we studied in *Habits of the Heart.*

In this powerful elite the crisis of civic membership is expressed in the loss of civic consciousness, of a sense of obligation to the rest of society, which leads to a secession from society into guarded, gated residential enclaves and ultra-modern offices, research centers and universities. A sense of a social covenant, of the idea that we are all members of the same body, is singularly weak in this new elite.

What is even more disturbing about this knowledge/power elite than its secession from the rest of society is its predatory attitude toward the rest of society, its willingness to pursue its own interests without regard to anyone else. Lester Thurow has spoken of the difference between an establishment and an oligarchy. Japan, he argues, has an establishment, while much of Latin America suffers under an oligarchy. Both are privileged elites; the essential difference is that an establishment seeks its own good by working for the good of the whole society (*noblesse oblige*) whereas an oligarchy looks out for its own interests by exploiting the rest of society. Another way of putting it would be to say that an establishment has a strong sense of civic membership while an oligarchy lacks one. One of the key differences has to do with taxation: an oligarchy taxes itself least; an establishment taxes itself most. In American history we have had establishments — most notably in the founding generation and the period after World War II — but we have also had oligarchies. It is not hard to see what we have today.

Thurow more recently has pointed out the growing disparity in incomes when an oligarchy replaces an establishment: "Never before have a majority of American workers suffered real wage reductions while the per capita domestic product was advancing." The real per capita gross domestic product went up 29 percent between 1973 and 1993. That was a lower rate of increase than in the previous twenty years, but it was still a significant increase. Yet that increase in per capita GDP was not shared equally: 80 percent of workers either lost ground or barely held their own. Among men, the top 20 percent of the labor force has been winning not some, but all of the country's wage increases. This is not a feature of all high-tech economies. Other countries comparable to ours, such as Japan and Germany, shared their increase in GDP across the board. And if we look at the top 20 percent in the United States, we will see inordinate differences. It is the top 5 percent that has gained the most and particularly the top 1 percent.

Together with the growth of this knowledge/power elite there has been the growth of an impoverished underclass. This underclass is to be found in the great urban sprawls that no longer deserve the dignity of being called cities, all over the world from Los Angeles to Calcutta. But it is also to be found in rural areas like Chiapas where peasants have lost their land and lead a precarious existence on the margins of an increasingly industrialized agriculture. The global underclass, as in a distorting mirror, reflects individualizing tendencies evident in the new elite. Here too family, locality, and religious belonging are weakened, not because of successful individual competition, as in the case of the elite, but because of a Hobbesian struggle for existence that is always only one step away from catastrophe.

In many parts of the world — for example Guatemala where 86 percent of the population is below the poverty line — there are only these two classes. Indeed, one of the features of our current situation is not only the polarization within countries but between countries. However in Europe and North America there is still a sizable, if shrinking, middle class, large enough to attract the politicians' rhetoric but not powerful enough to outweigh the influence of the international bond market on government policy. Given the significance of the middle class for modern civic life, the loss of confidence here and the growing cynicism about all institutions, including democratic institutions, is worrisome indeed.

If we wish to place the United States in this global picture there are some respects in which we are better off and some in which we are worse off. With respect to economic polarization, at least in the developed world, the United States leads the way. In 1960 American CEOs made forty times the average factory worker's income; in 1990 it was eighty times the average factory worker's income, and more recently it is estimated at one hundred or two hundred times the average factory worker's income. In 1959 the top 4 percent of our population earned $31 billion in wages and salaries, the same as the bottom 35 percent. In 1989 the top 4 percent earned $452 billion in wages and salaries, the same as the bottom 51 percent. If you look at wealth, not income, we find an even more skewed distribution. The most subsidized American is not the welfare mother but the Western rancher.

In tandem with the growth of this knowledge/power elite, as we have seen, there has been the growth of an impoverished underclass, the people from whom the elite are most eager to secede. Forty years ago people living in urban ghettoes could go to sleep with their doors unlocked. They were poor and they were segregated but relatively few of them were unemployed and relatively few of them had out-of-wedlock babies. They were not called the underclass, a term invented in 1963 by the Swedish social analyst Gunnar Myrdal to apply to those who suffered most from poverty and segregation. He carefully hyphenated the term and put it in quotes, and it was known only to a few policy specialists. By the late 1970s it had become both a term and a problem widely recognized by the general public and even recognized by ghetto-dwellers themselves. Although originally a neutral term used in social scientific analysis, it became a pejorative term, a way to blame the poor for their poverty. I wish to be clear that I am using the term only in its analytical sense.

As a term, "underclass" had the great advantage of being color-blind in a period when we have become sensitive about racial language. Yet for most Americans the underclass was a term applied primarily to Blacks, indeed to those Blacks who still inhabited the depopulated ghettoes, which now resembled nothing so much as the bombed-out remnants of the thriving communities they had once been. It is worth remembering that five out of six poor people in America are white and that poverty breeds drugs, violence, and unstable families without regard to race.

How could all this have happened and why did we let it happen? Part of the answer is the deindustrialization of our cities. Hundreds of thousands of blue-collar jobs, and many thousands of white-collar jobs too, have left our major cities in the last thirty years. Those African

Americans with enough education to enter the professional or sub-professional skilled workforce have been able to leave the old ghetto — not for integrated housing since housing segregation remains unchanged in most areas over the last three decades — but for new black neighborhoods and suburbs with some of the amenities of white neighborhoods of comparable income; thus the depopulation of the old ghettoes, which are now half or a third the population they were in their prime.

Those left behind were then subjected to the systematic withdrawal of institutional support, public and private. Middle-class African Americans took with them when they left many of the churches and clubs they had always initiated. Cities under increasing fiscal pressure closed schools, libraries, and clinics, and even police and fire stations, in ghetto areas. The most vulnerable left behind had to fend for themselves in a Hobbesian world where just making it through the month with enough to eat is often a major problem. Far from breeding dependency, life in the ghetto today requires the most urgent kind of self-reliance. Unlike some sectors of the elite, the underclass has suffered a crisis of civic membership not because its members have opted out, but because they have been pushed out, denied civic membership, by economic and political forces for which they are simply redundant. Other societies, less blinded by cultural individualism, are more sensitive to these matters than we are. In France, for example, the unemployed have come to be called "*les exclus*" (the excluded) and as such have become a central moral concern of the whole society.

This is not a story the elite wants to hear, and some journalists and even some social scientists have obliged them with another story, a story made plausible by our individualist ideology. The underclass is not, according to this alternative story, the result of the systematic withdrawal of economic and political support from the most deprived and segregated portion of our society. Members of the underclass have only themselves to blame. It is their resistance to all efforts to help them that has caused the problem. Or, in another widely believed elaboration on the underclass story, the underclass was actually created by the efforts to help its members, above all by the Great Society welfare programs, which caused self-perpetuating, indeed permanent, welfare dependency. The fact that welfare payments, including AFDC, have systematically declined in real dollars over the last twenty years, and that they have fallen by half during the 1980s alone, is ignored by those who tell this story, as is the fact that over 70 percent of those on welfare stay on it for less than two years, and over 90 percent for less than eight years.

The underclass story, which involves blaming the victims rather than recognizing a catastrophic economic and political failure of American society, serves to soothe the conscience of the affluent, and it even allows them to wax indignant at the cost of welfare in a time of expanding deficits. But more important, the underclass story serves to frighten and to warn all those who are not so affluent, who have seen what they have erode or who have had to battle just to stay even. The underclass gives people something to define themselves against, it tells them what they are not, it tells them what it would be most fearful to become. And it gives them people to blame. In the shrinking middle class, shorn of its postwar job security by the pressure of global competitiveness, it is tempting to look down at those worse off as the source of our national problems. If success and failure are the result of individual effort, who can blame those at the top, unless, of course, they are politicians?

Robert Reich elaborated this three-class typology of our current socioeconomic life when he spoke of our three classes as an "overclass," living in the safety of elite suburbs, an "underclass quarantined in surroundings that are unspeakably bleak, and often violent," and a new "anxious class" trapped in "the frenzy of effort it takes to preserve their standing." More and more families are trying to patch together two and sometimes more paychecks to meet the widening income, health care, and pension gaps that are spurring the "disintegration" of the middle class as it has historically been defined. In the anxious class the crisis of civic membership takes the form of disillusion with politics and a sense of uncertainty about the economic future so pervasive that concern for individual survival threatens to replace social solidarity.

In 1970 after twenty-five years of economic growth in which almost everyone shared, America reached the greatest degree of income equality in its recent history and enjoyed a vigorous civic culture. The challenges of the sixties were deeply unsettling but also stimulating, and a sense of civic membership continued to characterize the society as a whole. In 1995 after twenty-five years in which the profits of economic growth went entirely to the top 20 percent of the population, we have reached the high point of income inequality in our recent history and our civic life is in shambles. We have seen what Michael Lind calls the revolution of the rich and what Herbert Gans calls the war against the poor. A polarized society in which most of the population is treading water, the bottom is sinking and the top is rising in a society in which a crisis of civic membership is vividly evident at every level.

Robert Putnam has chosen a stunning image as the title of his article on civic culture: "Bowling Alone: America's Declining Social Capital." He reports that between 1980 and 1993 the total number of bowlers in America increased by 10 percent, while league bowling decreased by 40 percent. Nor, he points out, is this a trivial example: Nearly eighty million Americans went bowling at least once in 1993, nearly a third more than that voted in the 1994 congressional elections, and roughly the same number that claimed to have attended church regularly. But Putnam uses bowling only as a symbol for the decline of American associational life, the vigor of which has been seen as the heart of our civic culture ever since Tocqueville visited the United States in the 1830s.

Not only are there dramatic declines in the typically women's associations such as the PTA and the League of Women voters, a decline that gained momentum already in the 1970s and has been often explained as the result of the massive entry of women into the workforce, but in the 1980s in typically male associations, such as Lions, Elks, Masons, and Shriners, as well. Union membership has dropped by half since its peak in the mid 1950s. We all know of the continuing decline of the number of eligible voters who actually go to the polls, but Putnam reminds us that the number of Americans who answer yes when asked whether they have attended a public meeting on town or school affairs in the last year has fallen by more than a third since 1973.

Almost the only groups that are growing are support groups, such as twelve-step groups, that Robert Wuthnow has recently studied.

These groups make minimal demands on their members and are oriented primarily to the needs of individuals: Indeed Wuthnow has characterized them as involving individuals who "focus on themselves in the presence of others," what we might call being alone together. Putnam argues that paper membership groups, such as the AARP, which has grown to gargantuan proportions, have little or no civic consequences because although their members may have common interests, they do not have any meaningful interaction with one another. Putnam also worries that the Internet, the electronic town meeting, and other much ballyhooed new technological devices, are probably civically vacuous because they do not sustain civic engagement. Talk radio, for instance, mobilizes private opinion, not public opinion, and trades on anxiety, anger, and distrust, all of which are deadly to civic culture.

The only good news, and here, too, we may have to look below the surface, is that religious membership and church attendance have remained fairly constant after the decline from unnatural highs in the 1950s, although membership in church-related groups had declined by about one-sixth since the 1960s. My caveat about religious membership and church attendance has to do with the emergence of a consumer Christianity that may be primarily self-oriented and unable to contribute to any larger engagement. Nonetheless we must take what we can get. America's religious life is still our deepest moral resource.

What goes together with the decline of associational involvement is the decline of public trust. We will not be surprised to hear that the proportion of Americans who reply that they trust the government in Washington only some of the time or almost never has risen steadily from 30 percent in 1966 to 75 percent in 1992. But are we prepared to hear that the proportion of Americans who say that most people can be trusted fell by more than a third between 1960, when 58 percent chose that alternative, and 1993, when only 37 percent did?

Before we get completely depressed let us remember that we have a great history of civic engagement, which has allowed us to deal effectively with our common problems, and our decline is quite recent; therefore, it is still possible for us to reverse these recent trends. Furthermore, although things look bad in this country, if we look comparatively at our civic belongingness and even at our public trust, though down from our past, are still higher than in all but a few other countries. And most striking of all, comparatively, and even looking fairly good compared to our recent past, is our church membership and attendance (one would like to know if the 40 percent who attend church weekly compose most of the 37 percent who think most people can be trusted, but I have no data on that). The danger is that if present trends continue, our current comparative advantage will soon evaporate, but we should not underestimate our present strength as a resource for renewal.

I think there are two conditions that will make it possible for us to begin to deal effectively with our many problems. One condition is that we do something on a national and global scale to counter the deeply divisive consequences of the reign of the global market. As long as we are divided into overclass, underclass, and anxious class, most of us live under the threat of homelessness and despair. The other condition is that we repair our civic culture and strengthen our local, national, and global identities. To imagine that we can rebuild community from below while the hurricane of the global economy blows all around us is naive indeed. But the actions of national and supranational agencies to control the global market will not automatically repair our civic culture. Only initiative from below can do that.

Before continuing, however, let me express some rather dark thoughts about our present situation. We may remember that through most of human history societies have been divided between a fortunate few, getting almost all of society's tangible rewards and protected by state power, and a more or less miserable many. It is only in the modern age that societies have attempted to include all or almost all of their inhabitants in a democratic community. The motives of the elite for this change were not necessarily charitable. In traditional societies the mass of the population was engaged in low-skilled agricultural tasks; it needed not to be educated or motivated; largely it needed only to be controlled.

But two features of modern societies changed all that. The first was the wars that marked the emergence of nation states. Due to new technology these wars could no longer be fought by aristocrats on horseback: they required infantrymen capable of precision maneuvering and mastering at least simple technology. Then with the industrial revolution a huge labor force was required to man the new factories. Since societies required the active and skilled participation of the mass of the population in the army and in the factory, such people could no longer be excluded from society's rewards, and so we built the modern welfare state.

The problem today is that, with the new technology, most people are no longer needed: not needed in the army, where technological sophistication, not masses of infantry, is the key to success (see the Gulf War); not needed in the factory where computerization and robotization has replaced the assembly line. In short, besides the elite and its immediate subordinates, most people today are just not needed for anything except minimum-wage service jobs. The problem becomes again, as it was in the old agricultural societies, how to control them, not how to include them. And if this is true within the advanced nations, it is equally true between the advanced nations and the nations who are essentially left out of the technological revolution. The daunting task before us, if we are unwilling to return to a world of closed classes and mercilessly exploitative elites, is how to share the enormous productivity of the new economy with those who in the narrow sense are no longer required by it.

But let me outline a much more modest set of strategies for meeting our present needs. As I have already indicated, articulating a demand that our government take the initiative in controlling the global economy is the first priority. Many of us supported NAFTA and GATT with our fingers crossed because we saw them as providing the framework for international controls. We must insist that those and other international agreements actually begin to provide some protection from such things as currency crises, job losses, and price wars, so that our population as a whole can participate in our continuing prosperity.

With respect to our social problems, I believe the voluntary sector, including the churches, must reach out to all Americans in an effort to distinguish the real issues from those that express anxiety, paranoia, and xenophobia. However unpopular today, we must focus on the real problems of the underclass, those who are essentially excluded from our society economically and politically. We must combat the present shocking war on the poor being waged by the overclass and at least passively applauded by the anxious class.

Senator Daniel Moynihan, in a speech on the Senate floor last September 16, opposing a bill to repeal Title IVA of the Social Security Act of 1935, castigated the Republicans for proposing such a bill and President Clinton for not opposing it. "It will be," he said, "the first time in the history of the nation that we have repealed a section of the Social Security Act." The section being repealed is Aid to the Families of Dependent children (AFDC). Moynihan cites George Will, who was shocked that conservatives would take so drastic an action with no idea of the consequences: These are the percentages of children on AFDC at some point during 1993 in five cities: Detroit, 67 percent; Philadelphia, 57 percent; Chicago, 46 percent; New York, 39 percent; and Los Angeles, 39 percent. Moynihan went on to say:

> there are . . . not enough social workers, not enough nuns, not enough Salvation Army workers to care for children who would be purged from the welfare rolls were Congress to decree . . . a two-year limit for welfare eligibility.

Moynihan argued that "it will shame this Congress" to abandon millions of the poorest and most vulnerable children. I think we can say it will shame the nation. Yet, as Moynihan concluded, there was almost no voice being raised in defense of these voiceless children:

> You can stand where I stand and look straight out at the Supreme court — not a person in between that view . . . One group was in Washington yesterday . . . This was a group of Catholic bishops and members of Catholic Charities. They were here. Nobody else. None of the great marchers, the great chanters, the nonnegotiable demanders.

Of course the attack on AFDC is only one part of the current war against the poor, but Senator Moynihan is certainly right to focus on it for it shows it in the harshest light.

But we cannot think of the problems of the underclass without simultaneously thinking of the problems of the overclass and the anxious class, both material and spiritual. I hope you will understand me if I say that the real problem in our society at all levels is the need for conversion, which, in biblical religion is always simultaneously spiritual and ethical, a turning to God and a turning away from sin.

Who will speak to the spiritual problems of the overclass? The mainline churches may be in decline, but they are still in the majority in the corporate boardrooms, the highest levels of government, and even among the cultural elites, for if they are religious at all it is with these communions that they are associated. The thirty year critical assault on the dominance of white Euroamerican males in our society has not greatly dented that dominance, but it has been used to justify a decline in civic responsibility and a selfish withdrawal into monetary aggrandizement. In an open society we can work to make room for more inclusive leadership without derogating the contributions of older elites. I believe we need at least a portion of the overclass if we are to deal with our enormous problems. If the overclass can overcome its own anxieties it can realize that it is far better for one's self respect to be a member of an establishment than of an oligarchy. We can show them, I believe, that civic engagement, a concern for the common good, a belief that we are all members of the same body, will not only contribute to the good of the larger society but will contribute to the salvation of their souls as well. Only some larger engagement can overcome the devastating cultural and psychological narcissism of our current overclass. We must hope for the conversion of its members.

It would be well to point out that the majority of the people we interviewed in *Habits of the Heart* belong to the lower echelons of the overclass, what is commonly called the upper-middle class, however much they (and we who belong to the same class) would be uncomfortable with that terminology. Of course these are not the people who make the big decisions or who profit most from our current economy. They could even be called in Pierre Bourdieu's pointed phrase, "the dominated fraction of the dominant class." But, as we argued in *Habits,* they are the symbolic center of our society, their style of life is that to which most Americans aspire, and they do indeed prosper more than 80 percent of their fellow citizens. Their resources are far greater than those of other classes: they have the cultural and social capital and the civic skills to influence the direction in which our society goes. The question is, can they recover a coherent view of the world which will allow them to use these resources for the common good rather than for their own aggrandizement?

We have a similar and even more challenging task with respect to the anxious class, for its problems are not only cultural and psychological but sharply material. White male income has slowly drifted down from an all-time high in 1992 dollars of $34,231 in 1973 to $31,012 in 1992. Even worse than the income decline, in considerable degree offset by increasing female participation in the workplace, though that creates its own problems, is the rise in uncertainty. We are becoming a society of what has been called "advanced insecurity." Downsizing, part-timing, loss of benefits have become a way of life. Anxiety and anger generated by acute economic anxiety are easily displaced onto welfare queens and illegal immigrants. I believe they also contribute to the decline of voting and associational membership and even to the rise of divorce. While these economic anxieties are real and must ultimately be dealt with structurally, we can still make the argument that the decline of engagement in the anxious class only increases cynicism and despair, that a renewed engagement with the larger society, first through the church, certainly through labor unions, and then through civic organizations, is the most likely way to meet the very real problems that face society's largest group. And on top of its material problems the anxious class shares more than a little of the psychological and cultural problems of the overclass, for which spiritual renewal is the best antidote. Here the evangelical churches and the Catholic Church have the greatest responsibility and opportunity.

Meeting the problems of the underclass and attempting to reincorporate its members into the larger society is the most challenging task of all. The basic problem stems from economic developments that have simply rendered the twenty or thirty million members of the underclass superfluous (and rendered much of the anxious class only marginally relevant, we should not forget). Only a fundamental change in public policy will begin to alter the situation, and in the present atmosphere such a change is hardly to be expected.

But even indispensable changes in public policy cannot alone meet the situation. Where social trust is limited and morale is blasted one of the most urgent needs is a recovery of self-respect and a sense of agency, which can only come from the participation that enables people to belong and contribute to the larger society. Participatory justice asks each individual to give all that is necessary to the common good of society. In turn it obliges society to order its institutions so that all can work to contribute to the commonweal in ways that respect their dignity and renew their freedom. Not by transfer payments alone or the compassion of social workers will the problems of the underclass be solved.

In responding to the problems of the underclass, perhaps we need to turn to the principle of subsidiarity, derived from Catholic social teaching, namely the idea that groups closest to a problem should deal with it, receiving support from higher level groups where necessary, but not being replaced by higher level groups wherever possible. This principle implies respect for the groups closest to persons where they live, but it does not absolutize those groups or exempt them from the moral standards that apply to groups at any level. A process of social reconstruction of the underclass would require massive public resources, but brought to the situation by third sector agencies, local so far as possible. Today subsidiarity language, in contradiction to its basic meaning, is used to justify cuts in government spending. In truth subsidiarity is not a substitute for public provision but only makes sense when public provision is adequate.

All the churches that have a presence among the poorest and most deprived Americans have a special responsibility to work for these changes, but they cannot carry the burden without public provision. Ultimately what the underclass needs is not so different from what the overclass or the anxious class need. Its social capital is more depleted and its morale more shattered, but like everyone else what its members most need is conversion.

At the beginning of this century American Protestants looked forward to our Christian nation leading an effort to convert the world.

As the century closes we see that it is we Americans who, at every level, are lost in sin. In such a situation we might turn to John Winthrop's sermon "A Model of Christian Charity," delivered on board ship in 1630 just before the Massachusetts Bay colonists disembarked. In that sermon Winthrop warned that if we pursue "our pleasures and profits" we will surely perish out of this good land. What we are to do instead, as Winthrop, paraphrasing the Apostle Paul, put it, is to

> entertain each other in brotherly affection, we must be willing to abridge ourselves of our superfluities, for the supply of others' necessities . . . we must delight in each other, make others' conditions our own, rejoice together, mourn together, labour and suffer together, always having before our eyes . . . our Community as members of the same Body.

Under the conditions of today's America, we are tempted to ignore Winthrop's advice, to forget our obligations of solidarity and community, to harden our hearts and look out only for ourselves. In the Hebrew Scriptures God spoke to the children of Israel through the prophet Ezekiel saying, "I will take out of your flesh the heart of stone and give you a heart of flesh." (Ez. 36:26) Can we pray that God will do the same for us in America today?

THREE

Virtually Democratic: Twenty Essentials for the Citizen in a Network Society

★   ★   ★

David Batstone

A world is coming into being that is as different from the past as the industrial age was from its agricultural predecessors. A whirlwind of social forces will induce a massive redistribution of our economic resources, a shift in our personal and collective identities, and an upheaval in the rules that sustain our commonwealth. The tagline for these aggregate conditions are many, but none fits so well as "the network society."

The sheer pace of technological innovation in our time has been unparalleled. New generations of integrated circuits, though many times more complex as those of a decade ago, now appear nine months after conception rather than in three years. Nonetheless, to attribute the advent of this new age to a general phenomenon called "technology" inhibits our capacity to understand its true character, let alone chart its ongoing development.

Nor does "information age" do the trick, for the dramatic rise in the productive value of information cannot explain fully the discontinuities in our cultural practices. We have experienced for some time a wild growth in the dissemination of information across the globe. What the printing press meant to the European world in the sixteenth century, so the telephone, radio, television, and computer have left a deep imprint on the twentieth century. These tools of extension made our lives more efficient, generated a mountain of data, accelerated the exchange rate of knowledge, and diminished the stature of geographical distance. Even so, the stand-alone impact of these tools are now near exhaustion.

Their power is unleashed anew within a networked world. The melding of telephone, television, and computer capabilities forge a critical redistribution of information that within a decade or so will link together nearly all beings and all objects. Individuals will be connected without regard for space and time, and they will interact with machines with relatively the same degree of subtlety they expect from other human beings. This massive networking of the globe already has begun. While few of us sport silicon bits beneath our skin, Americans live in complex networks, globally distributed, which constantly transmit information back and forth across processing units, be they microelectronic chips or organic brains.

This synergy of intelligence efficiently links everything that is useful into a global network, and the results are exponential. The Internet is both a metaphor for and stimulus to that network. It took radio thirty-eight years to gain fifty million listeners, while television took thirteen years to reach that figure. The Internet passed fifty million users in merely four years, by which time the U.S. Department of Commerce reported its use was doubling on average every one hundred days.

The network society consists of many nets, however, not solely the Internet or the burgeoning telecosm of hyperlinked chips. Multiple contacts link the world's economies as well as its political and cultural movements. Money and information converge through a host of networks that are separated more by function than by form.

A largely decentralized capitalism is moving around the globe, resulting in widespread deregulation, freer trade, and an increasing prevalence of transnational associations. This wave of globalization exposes new markets for exploitation and expansion, and alters in unpredictable bursts the supply for labor and inexpensive goods. Within global markets, communications function much like the railroad did in the nineteenth century and motor vehicles in the twentieth century. They boost the productivity of trade, reduce its costs, cut inventories, and facilitate exchange of real value.

The network enterprise evolves as a virtual organization composed of many different types of agents. Mixed alliances of commercial, governmental, and nonprofit ventures do business with each other in ways that break conventional molds. Their collective systems, or nets, invest in new concepts or the means to create them, not necessarily in the machines of industry. Raising the system's prosperity opens opportunity for each of its constitutive parts. While production and distribution laid the foundation for industrial might, constant innovation and synergy within nets fuel the engine of the network economy.

These two broad trends, globalization and communications, force nation-states to restructure radically. The network society represents not only a new form of economic development, but the creation of an entirely different state of human affairs, with peculiar forms of social interaction and control. Rethinking the very nature of citizenship, then, becomes one of our single most pressing concerns. Unfortunately, most current studies of "digital citizens" are actually thinly veiled attempts to create a market niche. The real story plots the overarching transformation of social scripts.

Political ideologies that laid out the possibilities and prohibitions of social exchange within a mass culture mutate in unpredictable ways in this fluid environment. The network society lives off the energy produced by the cyclical obsolescence of social arrangements as they are outpaced or morphed into a fresh set of conditions. Information and synergy may be easy to produce, but they are extremely hard to control.

Changing rules dismantle old laws in nearly every arena of human endeavor. It sounds like a revolution, but it is not, at least in the apocalyptic sense of tearing down the old to establish the new. The "new" in the network society signifies a process, not a freshly prescribed order of affairs nor the coronation of a vanguard techno-class.

"We have it in our power to begin the world over again," said an enthusiastic Thomas Paine to his political cohorts more than two centuries ago. While such optimism toward the future permeates much of

American society at this moment, once again it will be entirely up to citizens to seize this historic chance to build a more humane and just body politic.

The following twenty essentials (in the spirit of Kerouac) for citizens in the network society admittedly do not add up to a blueprint for transforming the world. Yet they do offer clues how citizens will be connected, and lay out possible paths for their movement within a net. They outline political options and describe where they are most likely to lead. They identify the skills and strategies that citizens may need to succeed in any given situation. At times they even hint at how citizens can live with a spirit of dignity and integrity.

1. Community will not save you

"Community" has become the panacea for everything that ails us. The flower children joined it to usher in the Age of Aquarius. Self-help movements believed in its power to expel demons. Now new age democrats promise it will revitalize a country torn asunder by class and race. All to what avail?

Community implies a stability among personal relationships, identifiable roles and obligations, and practical activities that bind its members together in some kind of common venture. In our agrarian past, that venture might have been as simple as the struggle for survival, or as complex as the duties demanded by extended kinship networks. In the industrial era, community gradually came to be applied to associations who shared an ethnicity, a religion, a gender, or perhaps landed in the same labor pool. Hence, while communities once were known as sites that held people together despite their differences, their defining feature in mass culture became homogeneity. It was not much of a leap from there to identify communities as markets that bring customers together in one place, cheaply and easily.

Moral calls for a return to community become increasingly superfluous in the network society, albeit not at the same pace in every sector of the population. The institutions that once bound people together in small-town America — the bank on Main Street, the neighborhood church, the local union hall — quickly are becoming artifacts of nostalgia. We meet others today in transitional sites that offer services and relationships that address ever smaller parts of our lives. Those tissues of a self are linked associatively, yet rarely in a unitary way.

As the millennium turns, "net" replaces "community" as a meaningful way to name our existence as citizens. What matters are the forms of intelligence to whom one is linked, the practical support those connections afford, and the costs those connections exact. To place oneself in a net locates yet does not promise; associates yet does not homogenize; brings connection yet does not demand belonging.

2. Fight for your right to party with your guests of choice

Free association and assembly democratize the network society, and as such they represent an extraordinary challenge to the exercise of arbitrary state power. Closed political systems pay an extraordinary price in the globalized economy for restricting the freedom of virtual association. That cost escalates as the Internet becomes a prime artery for commercial trade internationally.

Association precedes commerce in a net, and plants the seeds for its later blooming. But association also delivers a flow of information that inevitably poses a threat to the orthodox belief structure of closed regimes. Once upon a time (not that long ago actually) the traffic of information could be controlled while products still made their way to market with ease. But such political strategies in a network society are equivalent to shutting down the entire transit system. Some regimes, like China, seem willing at the present time to make that sacrifice, though they will not be able to bear that burden for long.

3. Challenge systems that wield centralized and hierarchical power

A node refers to any point of intelligence that lies within a net. While electronic nets make the physical distance between linked nodes inconsequential, the distance separating any node that lies outside of the net is infinite. Put simply, if you are not a member of a net, you might as well not exist (as far as that net is concerned). The network society thus pits the collective force of citizens against bureaucratic systems that wield their power to limit connection.

A Peruvian provider of Internet services came into being in response to this very real danger. The Peruvian Scientific Network, known in Peru by its acronym RCP, represents the only electronic communications net independent of government funding in South America. Jorge Soriano, a journalist who founded the RCP in 1991, saw the Internet as a way to minimize the gap between the information haves and the information have-nots and to propel Peruvian workers into competitive global markets.

The RCP believed that to be successful it had to cast its net as widely as possible. A country where half of its twenty-four million people live in poverty, only 2 percent own a computer, and 4.2 percent a telephone, does not seem poised to leap into an information economy. To make matters worse, Peru's telecom monopoly, with the support of the state, hindered open access to communications.

But the RCP within five years overcame long odds by building value where previously there was none. It devised a creative scheme to position public Internet "booths" (think phone booth) in poor rural areas and neighborhoods, essentially connecting thousands of people in a rudimentary communications net. The RCP is now a major economic force in Peru, and has forced significant revisions to decentralize national telecom policies.

The tale of Chincheros, a small farming hamlet in rural Peru, exemplifies a net's potential. Prior to the arrival of the RCP in 1995, the village's income was just $300 a month. Once an Internet connection was installed, the village established a relationship with a nonprofit export firm whose mission is to open new markets for low-income producers. The organization arranged for the village's vegetable produce to be purchased in the New York retail market. Within two years the village's income has shot up to $1500/month.

Citizens gain leverage by joining a net, while those who remain absent to it are deemed irrelevant.

4. Don't count numbers; focus on adding wealth to the network

The well-trodden path to political influence in the conventional world of democratic politics was to win (or buy) votes. Then, suddenly, the rise and fall of poll numbers became the measure of clout. Bean counters experienced in measuring the output of widgets in the old system will be perplexed by the math of the network society.

As the wealth of nodes in a net increases, so does the political value of the net. But one plus one equals far more than two in a growing net. A telephone by itself is useless. Two telephones sharing a line create value. Link thousands or even millions of communication devices and the potential influence of that net compounds.

The direct mediation of human experience, distributed broadly and interpreted corporately, will produce more political clout than any single election. The beating of Rodney King by four Los Angeles police officers, one of the most important American racial events of the twentieth century, demonstrates that dynamic. The electronic transmission of an eyewitness's videotape, played repetitively on television broadcasts, stimulated more public debate and passionate response over race relations than two decades of congressional deliberation.

Whereas conventional democratic politics obsessed over partisan ideologies, net politics aims to build strength through accelerated civic engagement in the events that affect citizens' lives. The unprecedented capacity for individuals to interact so directly advances exponentially the political value of the process.

5. Don't be shocked by the future; learn to anticipate it

The heart and soul of a democracy lie in the feedback mechanisms that give citizens an effective voice. Electronic nets extend the amount of knowledge that citizens may obtain and the speed at which it can move. Constant change is an inevitable consequence of a society driven by communications. The speed of innovation dramatically shortens the shelf life of useful structures. Hence, while laws and public institutions remain quite necessary, they live in a state of perpetual disequilibrium.

The fate of organizations may not even hinge on their own merits, but on the fortunes of the nets of which they are a part. Junior colleges, for instance, were hailed in the 1960s and 1970s as the salvation of higher public education. It was widely anticipated that their flexibility of schedule and economy of scale would meet the needs of a mass population of adult learners. But today junior colleges are fighting for their very survival. Along came distance education programs and schools of professional studies, often aligned with major universities, to deliver even more efficient and convenient educational offerings. Despite the diligent fulfillment of their original mission, junior colleges have had to reinvent themselves or die.

Alvin Toffler back in 1970 coined the term "future shock" to describe the reaction of the citizen to fast-paced cultural change. Anticipation, which assumes trust in one's own intuition and judgments, represents an elevated form of intelligence in the network society. No economic formula or political punditry can predict the future, but the farmer who knows how to read the weather can anticipate when it's time to bring the cows back into the barn.

6. Make a political organization's tenth anniversary its last, then start from scratch

The network society does not just drop out of the sky. It devolves from the massive centers of social organization and economic production that rationalized the globe into customized cottages. The age of mass production yearned for predictable markets that optimized efficiency. The cross-fertilization of nets that communications technology facilitates turns that rationalized world into, if not chaos, at least more complex adaptive systems.

Decentralized nets usually adapt more effectively to evolving environments. For starters, they can more nimbly redirect their resources and overall game plan when change appears on the horizon. They also reduce the threat posed by sectors that resist change solely because it puts their own vested interest at risk.

Decentralization portends good omens to any democratic enterprise. So says the legendary American environmentalist, David Brower, who played a critical role in turning the Sierra Club from a hiking club into a powerful citizen's lobby, from which he resigned to establish the international environmental outfit Friends of the Earth, from which he resigned to establish the lithe but terribly effective Earth Island Institute:

> My rule of thumb is that a political organization needs to dismantle, or radically change, every ten years; otherwise, power accumulates in all the wrong places.

7. Push the process, not the agenda

The current U.S. political party system sits like a ripe plum ready for devolution. Precipitous drops in attendance at local and national party conventions and ever declining voter participation reflect its ill health. The definitive diagnosis: Citizens simply don't care. A growing number of U.S. citizens perceive, rightly or wrongly, that conventional politics do not touch their lives. At least political withdrawal had a political edge in days past: "Don't vote, it only encourages them." These days one is more apt to hear something like, "Really, when was the election?"

The current two-party system will not pass away any time soon, perhaps due to sheer momentum and monied interest more than anything else. But great gains will be won by that political party, or individual politicians, that connect their constituencies. What that means cannot be distilled down to new agendas, or even new ideas, both of which go for a dime a dozen. The democratic process needs renewal, not legislative deliberation. Citizens have to sense that their opinions, not to mention their daily life struggles, matter. They will own a process to which they feel they have contributed to build.

It is a simple political principle: People care more about those things they have helped to bring into being. Have you ever known a mother or father to care for someone else's children more than their own?

8. *Connections should matter more than computations in our schools*

The sheer production of information in the network society creates a daunting challenge to our nation's schools and colleges. We actually suffer from data surplus; information is manufactured in quantities far greater than our capacity to consume it. Practicing medical physicians, for instance, commonly lament their inability to translate to their clients the boom in basic scientific knowledge about genetics.

But schools will waste their precious funds if they believe investments in technology alone will pave the road to their salvation. All the computers in the world are not going to teach children, or adults, how to think. Education requires a renewal of pedagogy as much, and perhaps even more, than it needs new hardware.

The real engine driving the network society, once again, is not the mainframe computer, nor even the personal computer, but communications. A "wired" school best uses its technology, then, to open the windows of the world to its students. In the online learning site called the Global Cafe, for example, students from China and the United States share a virtual classroom. They read the same textbooks, write an "interactive essay" collectively, and produce digitized radio documentaries that illuminate the reality of their respective cultures.

Information is not only always power. Just ask any librarian. Empowered citizens need the ability to interpret and manipulate the system logics — both cultural and technological — whereby information is exchanged, and understand the implications of those exchanges for their own lives.

9. *When you hear an intellectual forecast the disappearance of work, assume that pundit has tenure at a university*

Historically, in times of great economic upheaval, doomsdayers seem to come out of the woodwork. The present moment offers no exception. A number of social scientists warn us that machines are displacing human labor at such a rapid pace that we are not far from a work-free world. Should we be so lucky.

To be fair, the restructuring of economic production does lead to the progressive elimination of industries and occupations that might have thrived in an earlier economy. Those conditions cause for workers a great deal of anxiety, consternation, and likely financial hardship. Agricultural and manufacturing sectors have been the hardest hit during the latter third of the twentieth century, for example. The economic churn of the network society promises to affect other industries in the early part of the twenty-first century. Very few citizens can expect to hold onto the same job, let alone the same vocation, over the course of a career.

The doomsdayers usually ignore the creation of new jobs yet unforeseen. Case in point, how many jobs were taken over by machines during the industrial revolution? Two centuries or so later most of us have no fears about keeping tedium at bay. A wealth of data in fact demonstrates that unemployment rates have remained remarkably steady, and perhaps even declined, since the end of the Second World War.

Jobs are not a stable commodity that can be protected. But a complex adaptive network ensures that tomorrow's work may not yet be born.

10. Declare a war on ignorance

Learning never ends in the network society. The gyrating movement of the economy requires workers to nurture endlessly their skills set and expand the sophistication of their knowledge base. High-tech leaders already have started to voice their concern about the dearth of trained workers in the U.S. labor market, a situation that will only worsen before it improves.

In his first inaugural address, Thomas Jefferson laid out certain "essential principles" of a democratic state, among which he included "the diffusion of information and the arraignment of all abuses at the bar of public reason." A strong democracy relies on its citizens to make significant decisions in court rooms, ballot booths, town hall meetings, army barracks, and newsrooms. But most important of all, the citizenry of a democracy must be sufficiently informed to keep all powers, be they commercial, legislative, or administrative, accountable to the public trust. Jefferson concluded,

> I know of no safe depository of the ultimate powers of the society but the people themselves, and if we think them not enlightened enough to exercise their control with a wholesome direction, the remedy is not to take it from them, but to inform their discretion.

America cannot afford to delay a radical reinvention of the quality and delivery of its education for its children and its workers. Since polemic can be cheap, three federal proposals that are by no means modest in scope are offered:

1. Declare a national war on ignorance, that is, a commitment to provide free quality education to all, regardless of age or social class;
2. Reappropriate two-thirds of the national defense budget to fight that war (the Cold War ended long ago, remember?) as well as a healthy slice of the capital gains tax;
3. Raise the salaries and prestige of teachers to a level commensurate with skilled labor in other information sectors of the economy.

11. If you want to live in a world without governments, go buy an island

Contrary to the dreams of more than a few techno-utopians, governments are not slipping away any time soon. In the interests of democracy, nor should they. The state has an important role to play in the network society.

Not that public authorities are in any position to engineer a social order, whatever might be the set of noble agendas upon which it would be based. How could any government, even at a local level, begin to rationalize and manage complex nets of citizens and the nonlinear churn of their economic markets? Restrictive policies are more likely to stifle the creative potential of nets to dissolve and regenerate.

The mandate of the government should be much narrower, yet more vital, than that of a social engineer: Maximize the infrastructure whole and thereby stimulate, regulate, supplement, and complement the initiatives of citizens. A government dedicated to the principles of democracy will strengthen nets, ensure fair access and competition in economic markets, and judiciously use constraints to protect basic civilian rights.

The primary impetus for state intervention should be the protection and promotion of private initiative on both individual and local levels. The same principle should apply equally to any accumulation of power, be it political or economic. One of the best deliberations of this concept appears in the modern social teachings of the Catholic Church:

> One should not withdraw from individuals and commit to the community what they can accomplish by their own enterprise and liberty. So, too, it is an injustice . . . to transfer to the larger and higher collectivity functions which can be performed and provided for by lesser and subordinate bodies.

The shadow side of the American experiment in democratic capitalism has not been the chaos of open markets, but the control and systematic exclusion of closed markets.

12. Discriminatory exclusion weakens your network

Although it will not happen overnight, race, sex, and gender will cease to be constitutive categories for defining citizen rights within a network society. Diversity has a salutary effect on all biological ecosystems, and human culture is no exception. Whenever significant segments of a body politic are denied equal access to nets of their choice, it weakens the entire net. Hence, citizens who are blinded by their discriminatory ignorance will themselves find little toleration for their beliefs. Intelligence does not sweat out of one's skin, but proceeds from the imagination.

Citizens in a network society learn a fresh moral discourse for social interchange. The Internet, for instance, is an ideal space to rehearse the improvisation of roles necessary. Virtual proximity to foreign bodies — who may not ever be seen in your own physical neighborhood — inspires us to construct, test, and transform the boundaries of the alien. As a result, racial blending and gender bending have become widely accepted in cyberspace, and these sentiments seep deeply into our cultural psyche.

The Violence Prevention Project offers one place for that to happen. The educational venture brings together an interracial body of students from court-ordered schools scattered throughout California, New York, Florida, and Texas. They gather together online in the Global Cafe to compare their violent pasts, share what triggers their violent behavior, and discuss how to prevent further violent incidents. They also learn how to communicate with their peers across racial and cultural divides, at times even crossing lines of rival gangs. The results suggest that students leave the three-month exercise with an increased understanding of each other. In the words of one student who participates in the Violence Prevention Project, "Violence affects everybody because death doesn't have any color to it."

The good citizen strives to make the American ideal of a more just and equitable union a far more common reality in the social fabric than it ever has since its constitutional profession.

13. Egregious errors of the past will continue to haunt us

One should not expect our immersion in the network society to miraculously cure our inherited social problems like a dip into the waters of Lourdes. The network society in many respects is ahistorical; it sets its gaze optimistically toward the future while ignoring the past. It does so with the same naive spirit of Herman Melville, who wrote, "The Past is the text-book of tyrants; the Future the Bible of the Free."

Yet historical deprivations will continue to retard the economic development of at least some minorities. A Vanderbilt University study investigated the prevalence of computer ownership and Internet use by racial groups. Its results indicate that black Americans are far less likely to use both computers and the Internet than white Americans. Perhaps those results are not so startling when they are correlated to economic class. But more disturbing was the study's discovery that a significant disparity in technological access remained even once adjustments were made for education and household income. If that gap persists, many black Americans may find themselves without the skills needed to compete for a new generation of jobs.

While education was lauded as the great vehicle for social mobility in the industrial age, in the network society it will be a matter of survival.

14. Believe in democracy, but don't look to the government to solve your problems

Despite sporadic gains in social capital, the American experiment with the welfare state turned out to be a dismal failure. As a result, most U.S. citizens have lost confidence in the efficacy and appropriateness of state intervention. Debates over public assistance now have turned into a zero sum game: food stamps or self-reliance.

The era of liberalism left us with this insidious legacy. Social benefits and political voice were distributed largely on the basis of perceived need. Being a victim, in other words, gave one a seat of privilege in the marketplace of public assistance. The system served in a twisted way to reinforce the helplessness of the "victim" who found "strength" in being weak (surely Nietzsche must be smiling from his grave).

Three decades have passed since Malcolm X warned America what fruit the tree of liberalism would bear. He was convinced that welfare ultimately robbed the recipient of one's dignity. If he were still alive, Malcolm X would thrive in a network society because he understood that social liberation demands personal responsibility and a net of organized allies. In his own day, he urged black America to create a net of value among its own neighborhoods. Malcolm X today could extend that virtual enterprise to Blacks in cities and towns across the United States, and likely to economic nets in Africa.

The old political logic that pitted Martin Luther King against Malcolm X, cultural integration against cultural autonomy, has lost its relevance. The reach of global networks are so pervasive, so penetrating, that ideals of cultural autonomy become little more than a fantasy. The network society, on the other hand, does reward political strategies that creatively link new nodes and weave those circles into a web of cooperative interest and influence. Recent economic jargon refers to such groups as "virtuous circles." A logic of paradox prevails: Diversity is rewarded, while atomized nodes that are bereft of their own identity, whether ascribed or constructed, are absorbed into the network wholesale.

The good citizen in a network society believes in unlimited social opportunity, but expects others to act on those opportunities with personal responsibility and self-dignity.

15. The flow of information should not move solely in one direction

The freer flow of information and the more sophisticated means for obtaining it frequently raise concerns about the future of privacy rights. Most citizens likely would be surprised to know how extensive a profile could be compiled on their personal lives starting solely with a home address or social security number. No legislation will have the teeth to prevent the dissemination of such personal information once it has been disclosed.

Rather than obsess about what others may know, citizens ought to be more concerned about the shared transparency of information. Near his death, legendary Beat poet Allen Ginsberg made such a plea for complete and open access to information: "I'm happy for the government to know everything about me as long as I have free access to anything that is going on in their lives and their political alliances." The million-dollar question is, if surveillance and data collection are unavoidable, who will have access to the data?

For some time, civil rights activists have fought arduously to pass "right-to-know" laws at state and national levels, primarily to expose state policies that had been made in secret. These laws in theory made the information available to anyone. In reality, the bureaucracy for obtaining that information was so cumbersome that only the most dogged political activist could get at it.

The Internet now makes that information readily accessible in a way that empowers citizens to become a force for corporate and state accountability. The Scorecard, a web site launched in 1998 by the Environmental Defense Fund, provides one such model for effective citizen action. Industrial plants nationwide are required by law to report the type and amount of chemicals that their facilities emit into the air, water, and landfills. At the Scorecard site, citizens can access that data by zip code, or even use a U.S. map to zoom in on detailed streets and neighborhoods. Scorecard users also are given the option of sending a free fax — form letters are provided — to the plant manager of an offending company located in their region. As environmental activists learned long ago, public humiliation can be an effective tool for reducing pollution.

16. If you don't like the news, go out and make your own

A world of new media has emerged that rewrites the rules of mass communication. The key additional element is interactivity. All previous forms of media assumed a world divided into consumers and producers: writers and readers, entertainers and audiences, broadcasters and viewers. Nets of communications now give everyone the tools to share their stories, in essence, to become both consumer and producer simultaneously.

This redistribution of media resources suggests staggering implications for politics. In theory, it means that tens of millions of widely dispersed citizens can receive the unmediated information they need to carry out the business of government themselves. Old media will not disappear from the scene, but their power to shape public opinion is reduced drastically.

A fun night out once meant going to the movies. Now it may mean staying at home and directing your own film. Advances in digital technology, especially the relative low cost and ease-of-use of film editing software and high-quality special effects, open the door for even amateurs to make near broadcast quality productions. Since digital films do not need to recoup exorbitant capital investments, they can be distributed to niche markets, starting with family and friends.

But why stop there? Due to the global reach of the Internet, it's fairly accurate to say that the home-produced film has the same international distribution potential as a Hollywood movie. Only marketing now separates the big fish from the little guppies. Then again, you have to stop and think whether anyone except your mother wants to see your ugly mug on the screen for more than fifteen seconds. Trust me, making the film is the easy bit. Convincing Uma Thurman to drop on by for a shoot is as tough as it ever was.

17. History has not come to an end, but it has reached a point of major transition

Global communication nets extend the range of what can be defined as capital and accelerate the pace at which it can move. Entire cultures previously distanced by geography and time will increase their interactions. Even the most isolated villages can trade the value of what they know and do. Small-scale artisans and consumers will find sites of exchange in the global market as was done on a local level at the dawn of industrialized economies. Massive wealth redistribution therefore will happen on an unprecedented scale.

Capital will not accumulate in the hands of a few in the global economy, but neither will it bring prosperity to all. Technology impacts not only individual nodes within a net, but it also structures relations within and across nets. The current global reality suggests that technology penetrates all countries, all territories, and all hamlets, but does so unevenly. The peasant woman in China whose body is subject to forced sterilization and whose labor is tied to basic grains may never use a personal computer in her lifetime, but her sense of self is nonetheless inexorably linked to developments in technology. The global economy, then, moves over distributed centers of technical power and complex degrees of periphery.

In sum, the network society will not usher in an era of utopia. It will initiate a radically new productive potential for global cultures, to be sure. But it will not resolve the perennial shame of rich and poor, standing side-by-side.

18. *Your grandchildren will carry two passports*

The conventional idea of the good citizen assumes allegiance to the nation-state. That notion will change in a network society as more and more individuals immerse themselves in international nets. The links they forge will range from marriages to commercial joint ventures, usenet groups to political alliances. These globally linked citizens will not be so swayed by political rhetoric asking them to put their nation first, e.g., "Buy American and keep our jobs here!" They may even put the welfare of some other nation-state on a par with their own.

These globally connected citizens will find worthy adversaries in citizens who are entrenched in more local nets. Nation-state citizens often view globalization as a real threat to their own economic security and cultural autonomy. When nets of which they are a part diversify and devolve, they experience it as fragmentation. For that reason, they tend to favor strong anti-immigration laws and oppose multination free trade agreements. In some states of the Union, such as California and Texas, they even seek to eliminate all forms of bilingual education. In short, nation-state citizens react like their world is under siege.

History is on the side of globally linked citizens, even if the political backlash against globalized nets will persist for some time. In the network society, borders are permeable, regulations are malleable.

19. *We will all become environmentalists*

Defining and controlling the environment, be it physical or virtual, promises to be a matter of fierce competition in the twenty-first century. Economies, natural resources, waste disposal, race and gender relations, modes of communication and "truth" are all highly contingent on the constraints and arrangements of environment. Most citizens already realize that laws and ordinances shape the contours of their social landscape, and as such require close democratic scrutiny.

But citizens may be less aware of how technological standards predispose net environments. Here the limits are set not by territory nor qualifications of membership, but by the limits of actual communication. "Whoever determines what technologies mean will control not merely the technology market, but thought itself," advises Allucquère Stone, who has conducted extensive sociological research on virtual nets at the University of Texas at Austin. Intelligence, despite the finer attributes that we accord it, is very closely related to information and particularly to its processing.

Because the flow of information is so crucial in the network society, the interfaces and underlying code that make information visible are powerful social forces. Wealth and privilege accrue to those who normalize the communications systems (cf., Microsoft since the early 1980s). These tools shape our lives as much as laws do, and therefore must be held to the same civic vigilance to ensure our social freedom.

20. What is past is prologue

"Imagine, my dear friend, if you can," Alexis de Tocqueville wrote back to France early in the nineteenth century,

> a society formed of all the nations of the world . . . people having different languages, beliefs, opinions: In a word, a society without roots, without memories, without prejudices, without routines, without common ideas, without a national character, yet a hundred times happier than our own.

Over the course of his lengthy stay in America, Tocqueville found an answer to his search. Civic participation, he concluded, served as the young nation's teacher and unifier. "It is because everyone in his sphere takes an active part in the government of the society."

The citizens of early America might not recognize the complex system of representative democracy that we have in place today. Our massive system of government has very little in common with their own intimate, face-to-face form of civic involvement. But emerging nets now make it possible to revive some of the essential characteristics of that early form of democratic polis. Multiple points of contact facilitate widespread dissemination of information and sophisticated levels of political participation.

The virtuality of these nets should not be underestimated. They afford every citizen the chance to place their concerns on the public agenda and directly engage policy makers and their fellow citizens in civic debate. But whether that future burns bright depends entirely upon the commitment of its citizens to uphold certain virtues: freedom of conscience, freedom of speech, freedom to realize one's talents, freedom of imagination, freedom from arbitrary power, freedom to associate, and freedom to dissent.

The United States has never been anything but virtually democratic, of course. American ideals have been applied only sporadically. Each wave of new immigrants, once excluded, only found a seat at the table after long years of hardship. Accounts of their struggles represent our country's greatest shame and glory, all at once. The American story remains an open canvas, virtually democratic, its future limited only by the scope of its collective imagination and the will of its citizens.

FOUR

The Crime of Innocence

★   ★   ★

Barbara Christian

The web that weaves ethics, cultural identity, and politics is highly complex. I know because I live amid the contradictions.

I was born in the Virgin Islands and, hence, am a U.S. citizen. At the same time, I am an immigrant. I lived most of my adult years as a black woman in the continental United States, but my culture is that of a West Indian.

I am an academic whose work focuses on black women's writings, a new field that came out of the 1960s' struggles over education. I teach at a university where there are large numbers of diverse ethnic and racial groups, from what is called "white" through the "four food groups" — black, red, brown, and yellow — to mixed races. Central to my intellectual reach is the intersection of the overworked trinity: class, race and gender.

I am a single black mother, the mother of a daughter of this generation who, like many of her friends, is worried about her future. A list of the items that trouble both her and me looks like this:

1. The vast majority of resources in this nation are owned by a small percentage of the population. In this society, being rich or poor determines one's housing, education, health, and general standard of living. For that matter, financial status determines whether one is deemed a criminal, is imprisoned, or killed by the State. More troubling still, the gap between rich and poor is getting wider. Yet,

regardless of whether people be poor or middle class, this is a nation that is inclined to have great respect for the rich and to blame its woes on poor people.

2. While it is clear that being elected is a measure of how much money one has or can get from others, this is a nation that pretends to be a democracy. But are elections democratic in this country or are they primarily a contest of oligarchies?

3. This is a nation that is waging an attack on its poor. *The Bell Curve* has instructed us that the core of our society's problem is the black or brown, single, teenage, welfare mother with big hips who is propagating at an enormous rate and who is producing inferior children. Yet, this is also a nation where, to quote legal scholar Patricia Williams,

> Welfare to single mothers constitutes 1 percent of the federal budget, 3 percent if food stamps are added. Only 38 percent of AFDC recipients are African American. Of all welfare households, only 8.1 percent are headed by teenagers. Fifty-two percent of those teenagers are nineteen years old; 31 percent are eighteen. Less than 1.2 percent of all AFDC mothers are minors (under eighteen). Further, more studies indicate that approximately 50 percent of women in homeless shelters and 60 percent of all poor women are poor for reasons associated with their having left abusive relationships (*The Rooster's Egg*, p. 7).

4. This is a nation that pays homage to its children as its future. Probably more than any other nation, we buy books and listen to talk shows about how to raise and nurture our children. Yet this is also a nation that cares little about poor children, finds it difficult to support educational institutions, and generally characterizes young people, not adults, as being the cause of many of the evils of the society.

5. According to anti-affirmative action proponents, sexism and racism have disappeared in this nation. Yet, this is a nation in which our inner cities are decaying, glass ceilings exist for women and people

of color, and 95 percent of all senior management positions are held by white men. In this society, white men actually can believe that they are losing while everybody else is winning.

6. This is a nation that proclaims itself the champion of women's rights and reviles other nations for their backwardness, yet practices an unprecedented rate of violence against women. This is a nation which has never had a woman head of state but worries whether an independent, intelligent woman like Hillary Rodham Clinton is a suitable First Lady, since apparently her intelligence implies that her husband is not intelligent.

7. This is a nation of immigrants whose politicians are waging a war on immigrants. Though this country's wealth came from the labor of slaves and many immigrant groups, we now believe immigrants cost too much and take away jobs from Americans, jobs that "real" Americans do not want. Though immigrants come from Ireland, Canada, as well as Mexico and Asia, the standard image of an immigrant in this country is a person of color. In a world where one can reach any continent in a day or, at the most, two, where one can use an ATM card to retrieve money from a bank in another country, many American citizens believe we should put up a wall around this country.

8. While paying lip service to the decline of the environment and noting that resources on which we depend for our existence are finite, this nation continues to sop up a vastly disproportionate percentage of the world's goods. This nation continues to exist on profit as the bottom line yet reviles other nations, from whom those resources come, for having such a low standard of living.

9. This is a nation whose citizens tend to know the names of their city's football players better than they do their own members of Congress. The citizens of this society seem so completely disaffected from the political system that a large percentage of them do not vote. Those who do vote tend to believe that, contrary to the facts, welfare and foreign aid, rather than the military budget, command the nation's largest expenditures.

10. This is a nation with possibly the most sophisticated system of information ever in the history of the world, yet whose citizens feel

disconnected from each other. Monopolized by a small number of companies, television stations have increased by leaps and bounds, yet there is little diversity of points of view in relation to race, class, gender, religion, or sexual preference. Though we live in the age of information, talk radio and TV talk shows spew out hate language. Words like "scum bags," "pansies," "animals," "niggers," "jerks," and "criminals" are regularly heard on the airwaves, not to mention a plethora of misinformation on a scale that barely could have been imagined a decade ago. Whoever is seen as the other, as being different from some imaginary norm that excludes most Americans, is characterized as being un-American. As we divide ourselves up into un-American parts, one wonders who is left to be an American.

11. Language is one important way through which we discuss ideas, come closer to reality, and clarify our thinking. This is a nation in which public discourse has become increasingly camouflaged through codes and cards. Welfare means race, a distinguished professor such as Lani Gunier can be bleeped off the TV screen with the phrase "quota queen," free market means free agent, the phrase "political correctness" can cancel out protest, and corporations' right to exploit their workers for as much profit as possible is merely "downsizing."

12. This is a nation that proclaims over and over again that it is number one and its citizens are entitled to the best of everything. Yet, this is a nation that puts more of its resources into prisons than it does into its educational, cultural, and artistic institutions. While this nation bemoans the presence of the world within its borders, it apparently refuses to admit to the impact of American products, cultures, and mythologies on the rest of the world, so that daily even languages disappear. Today the local invades the global as much as the global invades the local.

13. This is a nation that distinguishes itself from other nations as heterogeneous rather than homogenous, a nation that celebrates diversity. Our motto is, "The one out of many, not the many out of one." Yet, this is also a nation that appears to be terrified of all kinds of difference, and uses those who are different and most

vulnerable as scapegoats for the problems it faces. Our nation seems fixed on what poet Audre Lorde called "the mythical norm."

In light of this list of concerns, it is not easy to speak of a moral America and its citizens. One wonders if it is even possible to arrive at a universal ethic that could be accepted by all American citizens.

In his book, *Democracy's Discontent*, Michael J. Sandel, a Professor of Government at Harvard, states unequivocally that,

> Despite their disagreements, liberals and conservatives share an impoverished vision of citizenship, leaving them unable to address the anxiety and frustration in the land. If American politics is to recover its civic voice, it must find a way to debate questions we have forgotten how to ask.

Sandel offers a history of our previous public philosophies. In the nineteenth century, the reigning public philosophy was what he calls a republican political theory in which liberty depends on sharing in self-government and sharing "require[d] a formative politics, a politics that cultivates in citizens the qualities of character that self-government requires."

At the turn of the century, the public philosophy of republican theory was threatened by the

> concentration of power amassed by giant corporations and the erosion of those traditional forms of authority and community that had governed the lives of most Americans through the first century of the republic.

As is true today, Americans at the turn of the century experienced a moral, political, and economic crisis. Despite, or because of, the technological advances of that era — the telephone, the telegraph, the railroad, the daily newspaper — Americans felt disconnected and seemed to lack "sufficient moral and civic cohesiveness to govern according to a shared vision of the common life."

The result was the rise of Theodore Roosevelt's "New Nationalism," designed to regulate big business by increasing the strength of the national government. As corporations increased in power, a new public philosophy emerged, what Sandel terms the neutralized liberal approach to freedom, or the "procedural republic." The central idea of that philosophy is that

> government should not affirm, through its policies or laws, any particular conception of the good life; instead it should provide a neutral framework of rights within which people can choose their own values and ends.

Rather than liberty depending on "our capacity as *citizens* to share in shaping the forces that govern our collective destiny," it now depended on "our capacity as *persons* to choose our values and ends for ourselves." Debates between and within political parties therefore now focus on how to increase opportunities for choice and, of course, whom should have the right to choose.

Sandel believes this is why fundamentalist Christians have a significant influence on contemporary politics. "A politics that brackets morality and religion too completely soon generates its own disenchantment," since "even as we think and act as freely choosing, independent selves, we confront a world governed by impersonal structures of power that defy our understanding and control." A neutralized liberal philosophy denies the need that citizens have of belonging to something bigger than themselves.

Sandel is not calling for a nostalgic return to a republican theory, one that was never put into practice for minorities, women, and homosexuals — those who were deemed different from the traditional view of what could be called the common man, and therefore the common good. Sandel is aware of what he calls the coercive element of the republican model. "To accord the political community a stake in the character of its citizens is to concede the possibility that bad communities may form bad characters."

Sandel's arguments are enriched by placing them in juxtaposition to the writings of Toni Morrison. In *Tar Baby*, her fourth novel, there is a shimmering and precise passage:

He thought about innocence there in his greenhouse and knew that he was guilty of it because he had lived with a woman who had made something kneel down in him the first time he saw her, but about whom he had known nothing; had watched his son grow and talk but about whom he had known nothing. And there was something so foul in that, something in the crime of innocence so revolting it paralyzed him. He had not known because he had not taken the trouble to know. He was satisfied with what he did know. Knowing more was inconvenient and frightening. All he could say was that he did not know. He was guilty therefore of innocence. Was there anything so loathsome as a willfully innocent man? Hardly. An innocent man is a sin before God. Inhuman and therefore unworthy.

The speaker is Valerian, a descendent of Germans who named him after a Roman emperor, the owner of a candy manufacturing empire who has retired to an island in the Caribbean, an island that is one of the sources of labor and raw material from which his wealth comes. He has just learned that his wife used to physically abuse their son when he was a child.

But he is not only innocent of that knowledge. He knows hardly anything about his two black servants, Ondine and Syndey, who have served him for more than thirty years. Ondine and Syndey do not even know the names of the Caribbean gardener and washerwoman who help them.

The novel is profoundly concerned with what we refuse to know. If Morrison's characters refused to be innocent, were to know that which they do not desire to know, they might face ethical dilemmas and may have to take direct action that might disrupt their sense of themselves and those to whom they are related.

What Morrison is alluding to in her use of the word *innocence* is its Latin root, *innocens*, which means, *not to do wrong*, quite differently from activity, as in doing right. That perhaps is one reason why *innocence* can also mean ignorant, naive, or like a child.

Innocence is often associated with the United States — a young, adventurous country, only two centuries old. Early twentieth century writers like Henry James contrasted the sophistication of Europe to the innocence of America. But even before James, pioneers in this country saw themselves as coming to a Garden of Eden and of being an American Adam. This idea of America as a Garden of Eden, before the fall from innocence, continues to gravely affect our public discourse. The apple that Eve ate bequeathed the gift or curse, depending on your point of view, of the knowledge of good and evil.

Ethics moves the question of good and evil, what we consider to be right or wrong, into the secular realm. Being ethical means that one is aware of one's own self-interest, that there are contending self-interests, and that there is a relationship between these contending self-interests and a common good.

Democracy as a political system based on equality is not possible without a system of ethics. In determining those ethics, it is necessary to have a discussion about what our system of ethics has been and should be. Innocence is unethical.

One popular understanding that Americans have about their country is that it is the leader of the world. Our public rhetoric often emphasizes that our nation is *the* virtuous country, the chosen one, an entitlement given precisely because it has been the keeper of democracy. In other words, America is the experiment in history that has succeeded more than any other in the designing of a free nation-state.

Yet, as Stanford professor Claiborne Carson reminds us, although the founding fathers realized

> that the United States was a land of racial and cultural diversity . . . most could not conceive of a democracy with racially and culturally diverse citizens. They assumed democracy was possible only when political power was in the hands of white males with property.

Not women of any race or ethnicity, not people of different religious faiths, not people of color of whatever class or gender. The nostalgia of the "real America" that politicians sell to working- and middle-class women and men did not exist, has never existed.

Patricia Williams points that out in *The Rooster's Egg: The Persistence of Prejudice*:

> To assert the notion of family as a deep-rooted conception of male property is, in today's bruised political climate, to risk accusations of polemicism. Yet the entire Anglo-American property system of transfer and inheritance rests solidly on historic assumptions of white men as rational contractors and of primogeniture as a rationale for their inheriting everything of importance (*The Rooster's Egg*, p. 158).

Who, then, determines the common good? While few "families" in either the nineteenth or the twentieth century meet this criteria of property ownership, it clearly is one of the values of the republican view of the good life and has informed our national goals. Today, it is necessary to find other ways to envision and energize our concept of the common good.

Toni Morrison argues in her collection of essays, *Playing in the Dark*, that though Italian, Germans, French, and Jews saw each other as distinct and separate in Europe, they became countrymen through the creation of a social identity that came to be called whiteness. Such a creation was impossible without the existence of its opposite, its other, blackness, those who were defined as not being white.

But, as Carson points out, "The Founding Fathers did affirm some of the values that eventually allowed for diversity within democracy, particularly in the egalitarian rhetoric of the Declaration of Independence." The tension between the identity of whiteness as implicit in being an American and the egalitarianism of the Declaration of Independence underlines the two views of nationhood that scholars have analyzed: The concept of nation can be based on race, that is descent or community of blood, or it can be based on contract, a community of consent. The United States seems to call upon each of these models at the same time, while never resolving the tension between the two.

The egalitarian rhetoric of the Declaration of Independence points to an important element of democracy, that it is not a static state but a process. Democracy is a continual process of becoming. Since the signing of the Declaration, social movements such as the black movement, the women's movement, and labor movements have sought to extend citizenship rights to people other than Anglo-Saxon males with property. Still, from the beginning of this nation, there has existed a tension between an ethic of privilege and one of equality.

In enumerating these social movements, it is significant to call attention to the very language by which we name them. One of the knotty problems we face is language that denies our multiple selves. For example, people of color are also laborers. For that matter, all of us are more racially and culturally mixed than we might want to think. As Alice Walker has pointed out in her writings, her descendants have been here longer than most Americans, for she is of African, Native American, and European descent. But she does not think of herself, nor is thought by others, to be what we usually mean when we say "an American."

The issue as to who is an American carries with it not only matters of race and ethnicity, but also of power. Ironically, without the presence of convenient scapegoats such a Blacks and immigrants, one wonders how the elites of this country could continue to explain to the masses of whites, those seen as real Americans, why there is such economic inequality for them. Carson informs us, for example, that social remedies, such as affirmative action programs, were not the creation of black militants.

> Affirmative action programs were far less costly and socially disruptive than were the massive social investments in public education and health care that in time would have made affirmative action programs less necessary.

Massive investments in public education and health care would have provided not only more equal access for Blacks, women, and people of color, but more opportunity for all working-class Americans. Such social investments would have moved us further in the process of democratization.

There is considerable dissonance in our rhetoric of national superiority at the moment. In a remarkable reversal, Americans are now experiencing fears about globalization, particularly its economic, cultural, and political effects. While we dread globalization, which we fear may diminish our status as number one, other nations all over the world have for many generations feared the Americanization of the entire planet.

As American workers fear the competition of immigrants in this country and workers outside this country, they withdraw into their borders. These borders, however, have *already* been crossed over and over again, bringing raw materials, art, and knowledge from the rest of the world to the United States, even as this country has sent goods, television programs, arms, food, mythologies, foreign aid, and other forms of "American ingenuity" to other parts of the world. Ironically, the great immigrant fear is from Mexico, the country that lost what is now California, Texas, Arizona, and New Mexico to its giant neighbor. The very Central Americans who are supposedly using up too much of our welfare were raped, shot, and bombed for the last century through the collusion of the United States government with their oligarchies. The global has been here a long time. Now it is traveling both directions.

Perhaps one of our greatest exports is our rhetoric of diversity, a value about which we are ambivalent. Practically every major city in the world has increasingly become racially and culturally diverse. At the same time, there has been a worldwide trend toward greater economic inequality and conflict among racial, ethnic, and religious groups in Rwanda and the former Yugoslavia.

At a conference on "Multiculturalism and Europe" I attended at New York University, a number of German, French, and British scholars wrestled with the diversity that is changing their societies as their former colonies came "home" to the Motherland. Where else would they look for a model but the United States, whose public philosophy is based on equality and diversity?

What they found in the American experiment, however, was not so much a model as a series of cautionary tales. We are a multicultural society and have been since the beginnings of this society. The question is whether we want to live up to the ideals of our Declaration, especially at this period when American wages have remained steady or declined.

We need to ask whether multiculturalism is the great threat within, or whether globalization is the great threat without. Some thinkers, such as Jeremy Rifkin in his book *The End of Work*, point to the overwhelming effects of technology and automation on labor. Rifkin argues that fewer workers, be they domestic or global, are needed to maintain or increase rates of production. As an antidote, he suggests that we invest in a "social economy" within which workers could be paid to protect the environment, organize community development and other activities designed to nurture the common good.

Some cultural critics suggest the opposite, that technologies and globalization will create new and different jobs, and therefore what is needed is the emergence of a global citizenship. Sandel reports, for instance, that the Commission on Global Governance, a group of twenty-eight officials from around the world, published in 1985 a report calling for greater authority for international institutions and for a "broad acceptance of global civic ethics to deal with global environmental issues, trade, finance and economic development." But, as Sandel adds, while we need such organizations, such global entities will not heal our civic life, which is the touchstone of democracy.

My fear is that the threat of globalization diverts Americans from the ways in which we all participate in "the crime of innocence." We are afraid of being guilty of the crime of knowledge, of the ethical dilemmas such knowledge engenders, and of the direct action it may call upon us as human beings to perform.

It is within this context that the struggles over multicultural education is vital. The classes I teach at Berkeley are like the United Nations — filled with students from a range of ethnic backgrounds, although most of them are Americans. Initially, I find that students arrange themselves into the guilty and the guiltless. In not wanting to be guilty, they do not want to know how Mexico became California, about sexism and homophobia in black communities, about the ways in which the usual victim suspects are themselves sometimes exploiters, or even participate in their own victimization. They often do not want to know about xenophobia or their dedication to materialism and individual aggrandizement as a dominant ethic. In other words, they do not want to accept that we are all implicated in this state-community we call America. Ironically, many students do not even want to know about the complicated ethical achievements of their forebears.

One assignment I give students in a course on nineteenth and early twentieth century African American women writers is to interview their oldest maternal ancestor about their maternal ancestors who lived in the nineteenth century. First, they find out that their oldest maternal ancestor often does not want to talk about her life or the life of the oldest ancestor they can remember. Then they find out that so many of these women's lives are not at all what they thought they were — that they shaped local, sometimes regional history, even as they were shaped by it. Finally, they discover that their ancestors do not fit into the mythical norm of what it means to be an American — they suffered, had skeletons in the closet.

Students struggle through their habits of judging pain on a hierarchical scale, struggle through their sense of what it means to be a success, even at the expense of others. As a result, students engage in a world-wide, inclusive ethnic conversation. Such dialogue is what we need to make our democracy thrive, politically, socially, and culturally.

We are at a critical point in history in the United States. For many people the American dream no longer exists. This identity crisis leads us to ask ourselves profound questions. Do we trust ourselves sufficiently to acknowledge that a few have too much and the many too little? Can we accept responsibility for what we know and do not know? Can we comprehend that the planet will not survive unless we pursue an ethic of social justice, knowledge, and understanding of others? Are we willing to ask ourselves what ethic informs our public life? Is it an ethic of equality and democratic principles or one of power and self-interest? Can we creatively use the ambiguities that differences among us and within us engender? Can we inspire the direct action that such knowledge requires?

The fact that so many citizens feel disenchanted with the political process gives me hope. No one believes what our politicians say. A vacuum waits to be filled. While we may often be guilty of the crime of innocence, we are also a nation of diverse groups that want to learn about each other. We have a vital tradition of social movements, of people's movements, that have achieved much for ourselves and others in the world. If you don't believe that, talk to those who lived under segregation, those who lived when the eight-hour day was a dream, those who were branded inferior because they were Irish or Italian.

The cure is to talk to your neighbors, with those who are different from yourself. We must insist on being innocent in the positive sense, as curious as a child, and yet as responsible as an adult in knowing that ethical issues are complex. We need a national dialogue about what our ethics are, a dialogue that is informed by the words of Audre Lorde,

> stop killing
> the other
> in ourselves
> the self that we hate in others

The Crisis of Values in America: Its Manipulation by the Right and its Invisibility to the Left

★ ★ ★

Michael Lerner

The crisis of values in American society became apparent when I started work at the Institute for Labor and Mental Health in Oakland. This organization had been created by psychotherapists, social workers, union activists, and community activists to explore the psychodynamics of American society and why people were moving to the political right. Many of us were from progressive communities and had a set of assumptions about who the American working class was and why people were moving to the right. We believed that people were moving to the right primarily because they were racist, sexist, homophobic, or xenophobic but our assumptions were incorrect. Instead, we discovered that this was occurring because people were in tremendous pain.

We had come from a left world in which we told each other, "Americans have been bought off by the consumer society, and because they've gotten so many goodies, they are so happy, they feel a desire to protect what they have, that's why they become more conservative." On the contrary, we discovered that people were unhappy and unfulfilled, and what was striking to us as we delved into their pain was the similarity of their stories whose bottom line was: "I'm unhappy in the world of my work. I'm unhappy about what I do all day because I can't see what I'm doing as connecting to some meaningful life. I can't see how my work connects to any higher ethical or spiritual purpose. I can't see how I am serving the common good. I'm wasting my life."

We had come to believe that the American working class, middle-income working people, were motivated primarily by money. We, the academics, intellectuals, liberals, lefties, the social change people, *we* were coming from a higher place and had a different set of values. That's how we understood why we were making the choices that we were making. But *they* didn't have those values and were motivated only by material self-interest. It was startling for us to discover that this simply wasn't true. This is not to say that the over five thousand people with whom we talked between 1976 and 1986 weren't interested in money, but often their focus on getting a wage increase was a compensation for a life in which people felt that their activity was meaningless. "If I'm going to be spending all day in a world of work in which I don't really feel that I'm being actualized, then at the very least I want to be able to make some money. This gives me the opportunity, in the few hours that I'm not at work, to find some realization for my life or some possibility of connecting to some higher ethical or spiritual purpose." The categories we had weren't adequate for hearing or understanding this information at first. Eventually, we reconstructed our understanding of what was occurring amongst American working people and understood there really was an ethical and spiritual crisis in people's lives.

This crisis, for most Americans, is connected to the absence of the possibility of connecting their lives to some higher meaning and purpose. At the same time, the very people who were telling us this were also saying that this desire for higher meaning and purpose was unrealistic and impossible. "I feel frustrated, but, in a way, I blame myself for feeling this frustration because it's my own fault that I have this kind of job in the first place. I've screwed up my life because I wasn't more together." There are a huge number of these self-blaming stories that persist throughout the American working class. "I did something wrong. I wasn't smart enough; I wasn't together enough; I didn't work hard enough in high school; I made this mistake; I wasn't charming enough; I wasn't attractive enough," whatever. People have complex self-blaming stories that they tell about why they don't have jobs that are more fulfilling for them.

Secondly, you also have many people essentially saying, "I know it's not realistic. I know that the world is built in a different way and, in fact, I want to learn how to adjust to this world. Part of my problem is that I haven't learned how to cope in a world in which the bottom line is not meaning and purpose — it's money and power."

People learn one central message in the workplace: Common sense in American society says to "look out for number one." "Take care of yourself. You are all alone in this society. Nobody's going to be there for you. You have to make enough money and power either for yourself or for your boss or for the institution that you work for or you're out. And if you don't maximize wealth and power for these institutions, you're going to be penalized and others will advance and reap the rewards."

The same people who felt terrible about not actualizing their highest vision of a good life were simultaneously berating themselves for not being more successful at the world as it is — the real world in which they were stuck. Over and over, they would tell us how they were trying to learn how to be better at the materialism and selfishness of daily life.

One of the bestsellers of the 1980s in nonfiction was called *Looking Out for Number One,* by Robert J. Ringer. People bought it not because they felt it expressed their human nature but because they thought they might learn how to do it more effectively. Over and over they were learning that what really counts in the world is how much you can maximize wealth and power.

If you work in this type of environment then you will bring it home with you into the rest of your life. People have learned to look at the world from the framework of the market mentality, which dictates that you access other human beings primarily from the standpoint of, "What are you going to do for me? You're valuable to me to the extent that you can give me something, that I can maximize my own advantages through you. I can manipulate you; I can control you. If I learn how to do that — to manipulate and control you better — I'll be more rewarded in the world of work."

More and more people look at each other as objects to be controlled rather than as the embodiments of the spirit of God; rather than as people who are fundamentally deserving of respect and caring by virtue of who they are. Indeed, we look at people and wonder "What can I get from you? How can I use you for advancing myself?" As these attitudes are inevitably brought home from the world of work, you find a rip-off consciousness that permeates the entire society

This rip-off consciousness is evident from the very top of the economic ladder where some people in the corporate world rip off the planet's resources without regard to the future survivability of our planet. "Well look," some corporate executives will explain, "I'm in this job to maximize profits and the people who invested in this corporation want the same. They'll fire me but they'll just hire somebody else to do the same thing. In terms of consequences for the future, well, that's not what this job is about."

This mentality trickles down to some small sections of poor people, who think it acceptable to rip you off on the streets or in your apartment. The irony is that the rest of society thinks it can deal with this problem by lecturing them about their lack of morality and values when they have the exact same values that everybody else has in this society. The only difference is that they are applied in more desperate circumstances.

As people feel they are surrounded by other people who are looking out for number one, assessing them in terms of what they can get, every relationship and aspect of life feels much less secure. People feel that they can't count on teaching their children any values because their children will say to them, "Come on. I know how the real world operates. I'm watching television at age four and this value stuff that you're talking about isn't what the world is based on." And the kids are right; it isn't the way the world operates. It becomes frustrating for parents who try to teach values to their children to find out that they are extremely resistant to it.

Even loving relationships are in deep crisis because every commitment is based on this market consciousness. We have a society in which people are constantly being encouraged to assess each other in terms of, "Is this the best deal I can get?" A marriage today is much less about commitment, support, and a sense of total solidarity than it is a statement of: "This is the best available deal for me. I have decided that given who I am — my resources, my level of attractiveness, my charm, etc. — that this is the best deal I can cut." If that becomes what marriages and relationships are about, then you're never secure because you'll never know if your partner will not some day be able to cut a better deal.

Many times in my work as a psychotherapist I have encountered people who tell me, "We're splitting up the relationship. Why? Because I found somebody who fills my needs more." There is no further conversation possible after this because what has been lost is the sense of the other as an embodiment of holiness, as a being who deserves to be cared for and loved by virtue of who they are and not by virtue of what they can do for you. This creates tremendous insecurity in everyone throughout society, insecurity that is totally real, not just a pathology. It's based on the reality that you have a 50 percent divorce rate: One out of every two relationships will end in divorce. And so the other 50 percent are saying, "Well, how do I know that it won't happen here as well?"

There's tremendous anxiety that gets created in this situation in which everybody is feeling that, "Okay, am I sure that I can continue to provide the best deal for my partner?" In that market consciousness in which everything is an exchange, the level of insecurity differs depending on where you are in the market of goods that are sought in relationships. For example, if you're younger, conventionally attractive, or wealthier, you don't feel this exchange as being so painful, because you've got some of the highly desirable qualities on the marketplace of relationships. But the older you get, the further you are from the conventional vision of beauty or the conventional view of financial success, the more you worry about this. It plays out differently for different people, depending on your own assessment of how marketable you are and that changes at different points in your life.

These dynamics create a tremendous crisis in people's lives, a fear that is well-founded, and is accentuated by the fact that this commodification of relationships is encouraged by the marketplace to get you to see other human beings as objects to be consumed, manipulated, and controlled. This marketplace mentality in relationships results in short encounters that are hurtful, disappointing, and lead people to build deep resistances to each other and to feel more scared and alone. That's the social context within which people are experiencing a real crisis around spiritual and ethical issues. An ethos of materialism and selfishness permeates American society making people feel isolated and insecure.

The Right comes forward and proclaims, "There is this crisis and it is not a personal issue. It is a collective social issue." And the Right is correct about pointing out that there is a crisis in families, in crime, in ethical values, and in being able to teach your children values. The Right proceeds to analyze that crisis in a distorted way by claiming that the cause of this triumph of an ethos of selfishness and materialism is the traditionally demeaned others of the society — African Americans, gays and lesbians, feminists, Jews, immigrants, the other. According to the Right, these groups have been pursuing their own self-interests for decades. Moreover, they have been abetted and stirred up in this by liberals using big government to deliver them the goods and so *they* have introduced the ethos of selfishness and materialism in this society.

The way the Right poses this argument is very destructive. When you listen to the various forms of hate radio that have become popular in the past ten years, you hear the following message — "You, listener, are not getting the loving and caring that you deserve. You're not getting the respect or the recognition, and the reason is because it's going to African Americans, gays and lesbians, the immigrants, and others. They're getting it because the liberals are ripping off from you the caring and recognition that you deserve and handing it to these other people."

The key that liberals don't understand is that hate radio is correct in the first part of its message: People are not getting the loving and caring, the respect and recognition that they deserve in this society. Because the Right and hate radio acknowledge this, they have a tremendous audience. But then they give a terrible and skewed analysis of why that's happening. What the Left and liberals have done is to conflate the correct part of what the Right is saying with the destructive analysis. In other words, liberals and the Left have assumed that the reason why people are listening to hate radio or moving to the right is because they are racist, sexist, homophobic, xenophobic, anti-Semitic or whatever, as though that was the motivation. In fact, that is only the result of the process by which people are opening to the Right and then they become part of communities in which that racist, sexist, or homophobic discourse is a central part.

Meanwhile, the Right is in this incredibly contradictory position. It has positioned itself as the champion of the pain that people feel because of the ethos of selfishness and materialism. Paradoxically the Right is the *champion* of the ethos of selfishness and materialism in the world of work. With regard to the economy, the Right claims that everybody ought to pursue their own individual self-interest, that every corporation ought to pursue *their* own self-interest, and that no moral responsibility should be imposed upon them. In other words, the Right is totally opposed to any government, collective or social movement that restricts the self-interest of corporations or tells them that they ought to be morally or socially responsible. The same Right that articulates this ethos of selfishness and materialism in the world of work simultaneously positions itself as the force concerned about the pain that people feel when they bring that very ethos home.

The Right succeeds in working both sides of the street because the liberals and the Left aren't even in the relevant ballpark. They have no understanding of what's happening in American society as a whole because they don't even have the relevant categories. Liberals and the Left have an intellectual framework that understands only two primary issues; material deprivation — economic deprivation — and the deprivation of rights — individual rights or group rights. This is based on a deeply faulty view of what it is to be a human being; namely, that human beings are basically individual self-maximizers whose primary goal is to have economic security and the freedom to do whatever they want.

This leaves liberals and the Left with no way to understand a framework of meaning, of higher ethical and spiritual purpose, and as a result they can't understand what is moving people and what the Right is playing on. They can't appreciate what's legitimate in what the Right is talking about that allows them to then manipulate legitimate needs in illegitimate ways.

As a result of the pain that people are in from the deprivation of meaning and recognition, it's extremely difficult to talk to them about anything else. What the Left and liberals are understood as saying to most middle income people is some variant of, "Listen, stop whining. You've already made it in American society; you have the good life already — it's only these others who are really in pain. *Your* pain is nothing and you're just too self-indulgent, selfish, and insensitive to know where the real pain is. If you want to be a part of *our* social movements, the first thing you've got to do is acknowledge that your pain is secondary or should be listed as twenty-fourth on our laundry list. The real pain is economic deprivations or political rights deprivations." Don't misunderstand me. If I had a magic wand and could eliminate poverty, homophobia, and other social problems, I would do it immediately. And if I was forced to choose between that and eliminating the oppression of middle income people, I would probably choose first to get rid of poverty, racism, and sexism. But I don't have such a magic wand; neither does the Left.

The progressive forces in this society can't deliver anything for those suffering economic and political rights deprivation because they have alienated the very people who could build a cross-class alliance that would help the poor. Instead, we have succeeded, over the course of the past twenty-five years, in telling middle income people that their concerns are irrelevant to us. They've responded by saying, "Okay, then you're irrelevant to us." As a result, we can deliver nothing and have little ability to care for the poor and for those who are most deprived of their political rights in this society.

We need a different strategy. A cross-alliance needs to be built, one that addresses the problems of middle income people as though we cared. I say "as though we cared" not as a manipulation because, in my view, we ought to care. In my view their pain is real pain and their deprivation is real deprivation. I believe that the spiritual and psychological needs of people are as real as other needs and instead of being involved in this hierarchy of who is the most oppressed, we should help people understand all the different forms of oppression.

This is why we at the Institute of Labor and Mental Health, after having done this research for ten years, decided to create a public discourse. We started *Tikkun* magazine to talk about the hunger for meaning and purpose, to develop what I call the politics of meaning.

What the politics of meaning seeks to do is to shift the definition of productivity or efficiency in society. Today's definition says that an institution or social practice is efficient and productive to the extent to which it maximizes wealth and power. But an alternative definition would say that an institution is productive or efficient to the extent that it tends to create human beings who are capable of having and sustaining loving and caring relationships and being ethically, spiritually, and ecologically sensitive and alive. By this definition of efficiency, we have in the United States a very inefficient society.

A reasonable first response to a politics of meaning is to say this is unrealistic: "Tell us of a time, Michael, in which there's ever been a society based on loving and caring. Give us an example of a society where ethical and spiritual sensitivity has been the bottom line — and yet you want to change the bottom line in that direction." I want to acknowledge from the start that this is not realism in the sense that we understand realism in American politics. What we're trying to do is similar to what the women's movement tried to do thirty years ago. The same kinds of arguments were, in fact, used against feminism, namely, "Tell us about a society in the history of the human race in which women have had equal power with men in any family." You can't. "Tell us of a society in which women have run the major economic institutions in equal power with men." You can't. It was extremely important and transformative that women didn't accept this historical argument and instead said, "But this is what we need for our humanity." They did not accept the realism of those who said, "Let's be realistic," and instead opted for a vision of a society that they could believe in. And the changes that have happened in this society as a result of feminism are significant and illustrative of what is possible.

On the other hand, if you look at the Democratic Party and at liberals who have been realistic, you will see that as their realism narrowed more and more to the framework of what was possible within the confines of pleasing the dominant corporate powers in American society, their politics veered to the right. The politics of realism has ended up accommodating a move to the right, not responding to it, and certainly not providing an alternative direction.

It is time to create a different kind of social movement in this society. A politics of meaning movement is markedly different than the New party or than any other attempt that one hears about in the Left to reinvigorate the old coalitions. We are about a substantively different vision of progressive politics because we believe that politics should be about trying actually to create a loving and caring society.

Talking in this way can generate a tremendous amount of resistance and anxiety and for good reason — over the past several thousand years, people have used words like love, caring, and spirit in manipulative ways. Although it's appropriate to wonder whether you're going to once again be taken in, we should admit that we're talking about the deepest hunger that people have, hungers that are being systematically thwarted. Unless a progressive movement addresses these issues, we will see our country moving further and further to the right over the next two decades.

When Eisenhower was reelected in 1956, it symbolized the triumph of the New Deal because the Republicans had embraced fully the New Deal agenda, even though it was put forward by Republicans in a slightly different way. That was the triumph of the New Deal. This is the triumph of Republican politics today that we're seeing in both parties. This is not to say that there are no differences, but unless there is some significant alternative being put forward, we are simply going to move to the right. The significant alternative cannot be the recycling or the putting forward, in a more articulate way, of the same old leftist politics because those politics haven't worked. They've been unsuccessful because they don't understand the spiritual and meaning dimension of human need.

We're at the incipient stages of creating a politics of meaning movement. For those of you who know the history of the women's movement of the 1960s, we're about 1965 in the history of the women's movement — not 1968. In other words, we don't have a movement yet but are beginning to put forward these ideas, and people are responding. Currently, we're translating what these ideas might look like in some practical form and in my book, *The Politics of Meaning: Restoring Hope and Possibility in an Age of Cynicism*, I try to examine what a politics of meaning society might look like. I invite people everywhere to join with us in trying to figure this out in detail. Just as the women's movement did not have a detailed plan for what it would look like to have a feminist society or a society with feminist principles, we are similarly at the very beginning of years of work.

Let's take an area of a traditional liberal program in schools as an example of what might follow from this way of thinking. In the sphere of education, often liberals focus on increasing teachers' salaries, decreasing student-teacher ratio in the schools, and making schools safer and more attractive. We're entirely in support of the liberal agenda, but in addition, we believe that schools should teach empathy and that this should be a criterion of success for schools. How do we accomplish this? Remember that after 150 years, people still cannot find agreement on how you teach reading most effectively. Similarly, it's going to be a process to figure out exactly how you teach empathy. Perhaps, at the earlier grade levels you'd focus on teaching empathy toward other countries and societies. Then, at the next grade levels up — fourth, fifth and sixth — you might foster empathy toward the traditionally demeaned Others of your own society. In seventh and eighth grade, you might start focusing on teaching empathy for one's immediate peers. Of course, the biggest jump will come in the upper grades when you start trying to teach teenagers empathy for their parents.

Teaching empathy in schools and discovering that it is important and equally valuable as learning other school-related subjects represents a whole different way of thinking. One might even argue that the SAT exam should be abolished because it judges all the wrong things about people, missing the kinds of ethical and spiritual sensitivities that should be rewarded in a meaning-oriented society. The reading comprehension part of the SATs teaches you to abstract from every morally relevant feature of the situation. It asks you to focus instead on precisely those aspects that are not moral judgments or that are relevant to ethics or feelings. Those things are supposedly serving as distractions so that they can see whether you're noticing the right or wrong thing.

The question emerges, "Well, wait a second. What about people who are getting all this ethical and spiritual sensitivity — how will they get a job?" We have to change the way people get employment, and one of the things that we're considering putting on the California ballot is an initiative that says from this point public hiring (after a certain level of literacy is established) should be based on the degree to which people can show a history of community service. Community service is a strikingly different kind of qualification to be valuing in American society.

Let's say someone has a minimum base of literacy. Is the person who should get the job the one who knows fifty more college board words than the other one? Is that what you want to be rewarded? Is that who should have the public service job, the public sector employment, or someone who has shown a history of caring and commitment to a community? If you start to reward caring behavior, then you start to move in the direction of a meaning-oriented society. Another way of phrasing this is to say: American society is structured in such a way that selfishness and materialism are rewarded, and loving and caring behavior are negatively reinforced. We want to build a society in which at least the playing field is level, and possibly tilt it slightly toward rewarding those who are more caring.

If we approach the American people with a different understanding of the fundamental decency and legitimacy of human beings, then we need a different kind of progressive politics. Ultimately this means recognizing that human beings are motivated — in part — by a desire to connect with each other, and this is one of the most difficult things for us to acknowledge in ourselves. It's difficult because from childhood we weren't taught to find recognition with each other and to be connected to some higher purpose. We were misrecognized and did not get the loving and connection that we deserved and we were encouraged to blame ourselves for it and to think, "Well, this is because there's something wrong with me."

When you try and be hopeful thinking, "maybe it could be different," you immediately come into contact with all those negative feelings that dictate, "This makes me feel bad because if it could be that way, I didn't get it. I didn't get all the loving and caring that I wanted and maybe that's because I don't really deserve it." You're back in touch with these destructive feelings that make it hard to more forward and it's much easier to say, "No, no, no. People are really screwed up. People are really just all selfish. People just want to maximize themselves, and this loving and caring thing, I can't take that seriously. It can't be real." But it's deeply real in all of us and, in fact, it accounts for why so many people will grab for it in irrational and self-destructive ways or in ways that are destructive to others. A progressive movement has to provide a way for these fundamental needs to be acknowledged, validated, and fulfilled in a healthy, non-demeaning-of-other way.

There is in everybody, including those who will be the quickest to ridicule the politics of meaning, this hunger for a different way of life, for a different way of being in society. It will be possible for people to change and live for their highest desires when enough of us are able to say when somebody says to you, "Ah, come on, people are just out for themselves. They're just selfish"; "Wait a second. It's not true about me and I don't think it's true about you, either."

When enough of us start to interfere with that discourse of selfishness, materialism, and cynicism, to challenge the media, and to articulate the values that we really want, we will have this kind of movement happening (whether it calls itself politics of meaning or some other term). When that happens, which I think will be possible within the next ten to twenty years, people will look back and say, "Oh, that was inevitable. In fact, I can write a sociological thesis about why it had to happen at the end of the twentieth century." Right now it doesn't look inevitable, though, it looks utopian — and I'm inviting you to join with me in that utopian quest.

There are practical political steps to take even when fighting for a visionary and utopian vision; the Legal Task Force is a good example of this. We are attempting to organize people in different professions and workplaces to get together with each other to discuss the following question: "How would our workplace look different if we tried to maximize human connection, loving, caring, and ethical/spiritual/eco-logical sensitivity?" There is only one rule in these discussion groups: Don't let in "the reality police," those voices within each of us that say there is no point in thinking too much in this direction because it's so impractical and will never happen. When people allow themselves to have this discussion with those who truly understand the details of their profession, they come up with fabulous and powerful ideas, and, in the process, become enthused with a whole new sense of their potential power.

A second proposal that we have is the Social Responsibility Amendment to the U.S. Constitution. This is meant to be a partial response to globalization and a way of requiring that corporations pay attention to the needs of its workers and the community. Its basic idea is this: Every corporation functioning within the United States or selling goods in U.S. markets must receive a new charter from the government every twenty years; that charter will only be given to corporations who can prove that they have an acceptable record of social responsibility as measured by an Ethical Impact Report. This report has three parts, one to be filled out by the corporations, one to be filled out anonymously by corporate workers, and one to be filled out by community groups that have been affected by the activities of the corporation in question.

The Social Responsibility Amendment gives corporations a material incentive to change their own bottom line, and unless they become more attentive to the ethical, spiritual, and ecological consequences of their activities, they will ultimately lose all their corporate resources. It will then be awarded to another group (workers, community, etc.) that can demonstrate its ability to run the corporation without loss of its productive capacities but with a better level of social responsibility. Right now, corporate executives who may wish to be socially responsible feel that they have an obligation to their stockholders to keep on maximizing profits without regard to the social consequences of their activities. If the SRA is passed, they will feel that in order to be fulfilling their obligation to their stockholders, they have to maximize corporate social responsibility as well. We are encouraging people to develop their own ideas about the planks and aspects of what the

Ethical Impact Report should cover, and how to formulate it in ways that will make it impervious to corporate manipulation.

As a more immediate step, we are encouraging people in their own local areas to put the Social Responsibility Initiative on the ballot. Unlike the SRA, which is meant to change the way corporations do business throughout the United States, the SRI has a much more limited function: to require that corporations that receive government funds be socially responsible. The proposal of the SRI is: All corporations that are seeking a contract with your local, state, or federal government will have to submit an Ethical Impact Report, and the contract will be awarded to that corporation which, among those that can fulfill the contract and bid low for it, has the best history of social responsibility as measured by an Ethical Impact Report. This only affects those corporations that wish to apply for government money, a totally voluntary decision on the part of a corporation. Still, this process will begin to familiarize our society with the whole notion of an Ethical Impact Report.

I believe that something like the SRA and SRI will become standard progressive ideas by the middle of the twenty-first century, but for the moment they seem very radical. Of course, one can be enthusiastic about the politics of meaning and not be optimistic about any of these strategies entering public discourse. Once you get the notion that the central public focus of progressive politics should be "to change the bottom line" and to educate people about a new way of evaluating what really counts, there will be hundreds of strategic directions, and I welcome them all.

What seems important to me is that part of this changing the bottom line must focus on a new way of orienting the universe. The Left has been part of the dominant discourse of the Western world, accepting its notion that the primary focus of intelligence should be on how to dominate and control the physical environment to serve human needs. However, this way of orienting to the world, while important and not to be discounted or abandoned, has led to an existence where a whole different side of human needs are being ignored: our need to be part of a world with higher meaning and purpose, a world in which our love for each other and our sense of connection to the universe is given a much greater place. We need emotional, ethical and spiritual intelligence — and that has been ignored by the Left.

We need a period to rectify the imbalances of the past few hundred years, a period in which our primary focus has to shift from mastery and control to the development of a different set of capacities: our capacity to respond to the universe with awe, wonder, and radical amazement. I doubt if any existing Left or liberal party movement or organization is willing to take this concern seriously. For those of us who wish to heal, repair, and transform the world, a completely new kind of party, movement, and organization is necessary — one that puts this concern at the center of its agenda and continually asks itself: "Are we helping to generate more love, more connection, more mutual recognition, more ethical, spiritual, and ecological sensitivity, more capacity to respond to the world with awe and wonder?" I want to be part of building that kind of social movement, and I invite you to join me.

SIX

Race at the End of History

★ ★ ★

Ronald Takaki

Several years ago I was invited to deliver a keynote address at a national multicultural conference in Norfolk, Virginia. Once I arrived at the Norfolk airport I caught a cab, and soon was engaged in conversation with the driver. We looked at each through the rearview mirror of the cab as we talked. At first, we discussed the weather and how this region was becoming a very important area for tourism. But it did not take long before the cab driver posed a more personal question: "How long have you been in this country?"

"All my life," I snapped; after a while, one gets impatient responding to that question. But then I calmed down and informed this white man in his forties, at whom I was looking in the rearview mirror, that my grandfather had come to the United States in 1886. I explained to him that we had been in this country as a family for more than one hundred years, and that I myself was born here. And then he looked at me in the rearview mirror and said, with a broad Southern drawl, "Well, I was wondering about you, because your English is excellent."

He did not see me as an American. I am not saying that he asked me this question because he was a Southerner, since Northerners have asked me the same question. Nor can I attribute his ignorance to economic class since, to be honest, Ph.D.s have also asked me this question. And it is not necessarily a matter of race, either, since African Americans have also questioned my nationality. I do not look American to a lot of people.

My experience in the cab mirrors a very common assumption that being "American" means being white, or European in ancestry. But one need only look around the streets of just about any American city to realize how far from reality this perception is. Many of us came originally from Africa, others were already here, others came up from Latin America and others, like my grandfather, came from a Pacific shore, and we're all Americans. Yet, despite that history, the prevailing debate about American citizenship revolves around identity: Who is an American and how does identity shape American society?

Racial and ethnic diversity is being promoted, and contested, of course, on university and college campuses across the country. In 1989, my colleagues at the University of California, Berkeley, voted favorably to establish a multicultural requirement for graduation. We call it the "American cultures requirement," and it applies to every student in the university. Even students in engineering, computer science, and business administration must take a course before graduation that is designed to deepen and broaden their understanding of American society in terms of race and ethnicity. The course is neither a cultural diversity requirement, nor a global studies requirement. It is a requirement that focuses on diversity in the United States of America. The curriculum is designed to study comparatively — and we underline "comparatively" — five groups, which we have identified as African American, Asian American, Latino, American Indian, and European immigrant groups, particularly those groups that arrived in the late nineteenth and early twentieth centuries from Italy, Greece, Poland, Hungary, and Russia. Berkeley today offers approximately 125 courses that fulfill this requirement, fielded by faculty in almost twenty different departments.

The Berkeley faculty instituted the American cultures requirement essentially for two reasons. The first motivation was intellectual, since we believed that it would bring our students to a more accurate understanding of American society. On a more urgent note, however, we believed that we were witnessing at the time the most serious racial crisis in America since the Civil War. Those fears were confirmed only three years later when, on 29 April 1992, we saw on our television screens terrifying images beamed out of Los Angeles: Korean stores burning out of control, black smoke rising to the skies above the city, and murderous melee in the streets. The most powerful image that came out of those events was the face of Rodney King. I still remember his trembling words, "Please, people, we're stuck here for a while; we can work it out, we can get along."

But many of us, educators and students alike, wondered, "How do we get along, how do we work it out, unless we learn more about one another?" The Berkeley faculty trusted that a comparative approach to multiculturalism would help our students understand the beauty and promise of a pluralistic America.

I am often asked by faculty, deans, and provosts across the country to describe what a multicultural approach to culture looks like. Offering a theoretical description is usually less effective than providing an actual demonstration. The remainder of this essay, then, serves as a demonstration of a comparative multicultural approach to history.

Francis Fukuyama, a fellow Asian American intellectual, proclaims in his book entitled, *The End of History and the Last Man*, that at the turn of the twentieth century the globe is witnessing the end of history. Liberal democracy, he declares, has triumphed over communism, and the capitalist economic system has emerged as the only coherent political and economic ideology. The overriding message Fukuyama offers is celebratory — the triumph of American liberal democracy and capitalism, the end of history.

But Fukuyama's conclusion that history has come to an end relies upon a very specific view of history. If we define history as the conflict between liberal democracy and capitalism on the one hand, and feudalism, monarchy, and communism on the other hand, then perhaps we would have to agree with Fukuyama that history has ended. Alternatively, if one defines history as the expansion of Europe into Africa, the Americas, Asia and the Pacific, if one defines history as the history of colonialism, if one defines history as a trail of racial and ethnic conflicts, then one would have to say that history has in no way ended.

Even Fukuyama would have to agree that U.S. history has not come to an end, for example, since racial inequality for Blacks is such an undeniable social fact. All the same, he does not accept any explanation that finds fault with liberal democracy for this state of affairs. He instead would frame racial inequality as a cultural problem for Blacks. In his analysis, black poverty is a matter of cultural difference. Blacks lack middle-class values of thrift, hard work, self-reliance, and family values that they need in order to succeed, he argues. In other words, the black problem is group specific and cultural. His remedy: the way for Blacks to make it into the mainstream is for the group to acquire the proper values.

Fukuyama's judgment of black failure is juxtaposed with his estimation of economic success gained by other ethnic groups. In *The End of History*, for instance, he notes that Japan's economic miracle is based on the richness of its culture. He compares the Japanese cultural ethos favorably to the Protestant ethic: values rooted in hard work, thrift, industry, and family. Though Fukuyama did not develop this comparison any further in *The End of History*, in a subsequent book, entitled *Trust*, he expands this theory that links cultural values and material well-being. He confesses admiration for the gains of Asian Americans in the United States; more specifically, he lauds the broad achievements of Japanese Americans, Chinese Americans, and Korean Americans. He again attributes the success of Asian Americans to their strong family values and ethnic enterprise, and pointedly notes that Blacks are deficient in these values.

In making these comparisons and contrasts, Fukuyama continues the long and storied myth of the Asian American model minority. This myth rests on the claim that Asian Americans have made it economically, and is usually documented by statistics which show that Asian American families have incomes that even at times exceed that of white families. But statistics that measure family income make sense only in relation to the number of workers per family. A close look at these numbers reflects that Asian American families typically have more workers per family than white families, which serves to incline upward Asian American family incomes.

The myth of Asian American success also overlooks a second important reality. The majority of the Asian American population lives in three states: New York, California, and Hawaii, with the highest concentration situated in San Francisco, Los Angeles, New York City, and Honolulu. These cities annually report among the highest cost of living indexes in the entire country. So, of course, an inflated index will incline income upward. Those numbers do not necessarily suggest a higher standard of living, however.

And there is yet another problem with this myth. It lumps together all Asian Americans, whether they be Chinese, Japanese, Koreans, Hmong, Vietnamese, Cambodians, or a host of other Asian immigrant groups. Such lumping together renders invisible those Asian American groups that have not yet made it economically in this country. Even within a group that seemingly is successful, say Chinese Americans, this myth overlooks the class heterogeneity within that community. In New York City, for example, wide class divisions divide the uptown Chinese from the downtown Chinese.

I am not trying to deny that there are many successful Asian Americans in the United States. But it is important to realize that many of them, probably the majority who are successful, are post-1965 immigrants. They often come from the professional and highly educated classes of South Korea, Taiwan, Hong Kong, and the Philippines. One study of Korean green grocers in New York City, for example, revealed that nearly 78 percent of those interviewed had college degrees. Hence, many relatively recent immigrants came here already middle-class and upper-middle-class. They did not pull themselves up by their bootstraps.

All the same, many of these professional Asian Americans complain that they experience a "glass ceiling." In other words, even though they may have degrees from elite universities, they find that they are not earning an income comparable to their skill level and their level of education.

But the point of this celebration of Asian Americans as a model minority, in reality, is not sociology. The debate between Fukuyama and me is not even about history. It is really about ideology, because embedded within that sociology, contained within that history, is an ideology. The message is this: The American dream still holds promise to all of us as Americans. Everyone, regardless of race, can make it into the mainstream through hard work and private effort.

The key word here is "private." Notice, these Asian Americans made it not through affirmative action, not through welfare, but through private activities — business, education, and individual effort. In other words, the way to make it into the mainstream, the way to advance oneself economically, is in the private domain, relying on family resources, not by means of government assistance.

As a historian, I have to raise the question whether this representation of Asian Americans as a model minority is a recent phenomenon. It certainly receives wide promotion from scholars such as Fukuyama, Thomas Sowell, Dinesh D'Souza, and Nathan Glazer. But it is not a recent idea.

Looking backward into the nineteenth century to just one year — 1870 — we find two fascinating examples of how Asian Americans were used as a model minority. The first series of events took place in the states of Mississippi and Louisiana. After the Civil War, following the emancipation of enslaved African Americans, planters in Mississippi, Louisiana, and other states in the South were confronted with a wage-earning class of Blacks. Often, the planters had labor conflicts with these newly freed Blacks. So in 1870, a coalition of planters transported into Mississippi and Louisiana more than five hundred Chinese immigrant laborers whom they pitted against black wage-earners. A review of newspaper reports from the period as well as written correspondence among the planters themselves reveal the clear intent of this importation of Chinese labor. The planters blatantly admitted their plans to use these Chinese immigrant laborers as examples of obedient, hard-working laborers. A model minority for whom? For the newly freed Blacks.

In 1870, another significant event occurred, but this time in the North, in a small industrial town in Massachusetts. The largely immigrant Irish working class of North Adams had organized themselves into a union called the "Knights of St. Crispins." These Irish factory workers went out on strike against a factory owned by Charles Sampson in 1870. So Sampson transported across the country about seventy-five Chinese immigrant laborers, brought them to North Adams, Massachusetts, to break the strike. Again, the local newspapers went wild, proclaiming, here we have the solution to all of our labor problems; not only cheap labor but obedient labor, industrious labor. Their statistics in fact "proved" — and this was later hailed by the mainstream media beyond North Adams — that after four months the Chinese workers were out-producing the Irish workers. In short, the Chinese were touted as more efficient workers.

The Irish workers of North Adams initially tried to build class solidarity across racial lines, even attempting to organize a Chinese Lodge of the Knights of St. Crispins. But Sampson locked the Chinese within the compounds, separated them from the Irish strikers, and broke the strike. That was in 1870. In Mississippi, Alabama, and North Adams, Massachusetts, the Chinese were used as a model minority for Black workers and as a model minority for Irish immigrant workers.

But then nearly a decade later came a nativist backlash against Chinese immigrants that culminated in the 1882 Chinese Exclusion Act. The closing of the gates to Chinese immigration occurred within a larger context, however. American industrial development had become overheated by the 1880s and production was slowing down. America "discovered" unemployment for the first time in its history.

A young historian by the name of Frederick Jackson Turner chose this important cultural moment to deliver a seminal thesis at the meeting of the American Historical Association in Chicago in 1893. The paper was entitled "The Significance of the Frontier in American History." Turner proposed that America's manifest destiny and national character were deeply shaped by the frontier experience. He hailed the westward migration of white settlers, and the expansion of what he called "the advance of civilization against savagery," a hard-fought victory won at the expense of the Native American Indians. Viewed from our present perspective, Turner's thesis could be very well retitled, "The Significance of the Frontier and Race in American History."

There stood Turner at the end of the nineteenth century, contemplating the social significance of the end of the frontier, and today we have Francis Fukuyama, contemplating the end of another century and the eclipse of that frontier he calls history. Turner idealized the triumphant advance of civilization across a continent, while Fukuyama trumpeted the advance of a civilization across the entire world. In the 1870s Chinese immigrant laborers were used as a model minority against Blacks and Irish immigrant workers. The workplace — the

plantation, the shoe factory — was a site of discipline, the site to create docile, obedient, efficient workers. Today, the site of discipline has
shifted from the workplace to the cultural terrain. "Cultural terrain"
refers to ideology and culture, to representations of minorities in the
mass media, but also to representations in our scholarly and political
discourse.

In the nineteenth century there was a need for Black labor. Today,
we are witnessing a dramatic decline in the need for Black labor. We
presently have what William Julius Wilson calls the formation and expansion of a "Black underclass" in our inner cities. Wilson identifies
two very important factors behind this development in the U.S. economy. He highlights the deindustrialization of America and the emergence of a globalized economy. Now our factories can go overseas,
our jobs can go to Mexico, to Indonesia, to Malaysia. This exportation
of production is hollowing out the industrial inner cities.

Another development that Wilson underscores is the suburbaniza-
tion of production, that is, the movement of sites of production away
from our cities, that began with earnest in the early 1980s. Not just
manufacturing production, but also information production thrives in
suburban office parks. Downtowns are rapidly closing down, leaving
the people who cannot move trapped in inner cities.

Jeremy Rifkin's study on the changing patterns of work in America
adds a further perspective on the formation of an underclass that is
largely Black. In his book, *The End of Work*, Rifkin shows very persua-
sively that while industrial and information production have both risen
dramatically in the last two decades, the need for labor has remained
level and in some cases even declined. Rifkin discovers these trends
not only in manufacturing labor, but also in white-collar labor. In
essence, our economy has less need for labor and so work is coming
to an end. Rifkin claims that the creation of superfluous workers in
American society will only increase in the twenty-first century, and this
problem is having, and will continue to have, a disproportionate impact upon African Americans trapped in our inner cities.

In the nineteenth century the purpose of the model minority was
to control labor. The function of the model minority today is not to
control Black or Irish immigrant labor, and not even to create obedi-

ent, hard-working laborers. The function today is social control, a reaffirmation of the American dream directed especially to those workers, many of them White and many of them Black, who are struggling simply to make ends meet. "Be like Asian Americans, emulate their family values."

But this message has a special targeting for African Americans who feel that their future is hopeless. It says to them, "Look at those Asian Americans. They were able to make it, they're shopkeepers, they're successful, they're getting their children into schools like Berkeley and Harvard and Princeton. And how did they do it? They did it through private activities, through emphasis on education, through family values."

Family values have become the code words for defining the problem of poverty in terms of the family and the individual rather than the structures of our economy and the structures of our society. Blacks are told to be like Asian Americans — be law-abiding, be civil members of society, don't depend on welfare, don't try to get ahead through affirmative action.

Many Asian Americans have inadvertently joined Fukuyama in touting Asian American success; in some cases even liberal Asian American organizations have done so. They actively promote Asian American family values, releasing sociological data showing that we have low welfare dependency rates. They also regularly provide information to the media about how we're contributing as Asian Americans to the economy through shopkeeping, through connections with businesses in South Korea, Taiwan, and Hong Kong. These liberal Asian Americans say they are performing these activities to resist racism, to combat the backlash against immigrants, to show that Asian Americans are good citizens, that we're good Americans. But like the conservative Fukuyama, these liberal Asian Americans overlook the social and economic structures that produce and reproduce racial inequality. In a complicated way, the Asian American model minority representation has become part of Michel Foucault's concept of the panopticon — society controlled by an ideology dividing us into distinct groups, ever being watched and compared.

There are major differences that distinguish the economy and society at the end of the nineteenth century to that we are facing at the end of the twentieth century. But, as it turns out, there are also significant similarities. Both periods represent times of economic crisis and class tensions among Whites. Consider the labor turmoils and strikes in the late nineteenth century, the 1885 Haymarket Riot in Chicago, the Homestead Riot, and the Pullman Strike. These events were eruptions that shook American society, and it was within the context of white/white class conflicts that this young historian, Frederick Jackson Turner, gave his paper. He was in Chicago, only eight years after the bloody Haymarket Riot, presenting this paper on the significance of the frontier. He was worried about his country's future, and his interpretation of the end of the frontier was informed by that larger economic context of an industrial machine slowing down, rising unemployment, and the emergence of white/white class conflict.

Turner was not the only person contemplating the meaning of the end of his century. At about the same time another American, Henry George, was calling for a radical redefinition of citizenship that would include shared ownership of the continent. In his book, *Progress and Poverty*, George argued that the advance of capitalism in American civilization would inevitably lead to more intense and violent class conflicts within white society. He proposed the idea of a tax on unearned income to reduce the conflict. Once land becomes valuable due to industrial production, then there should be a tax on the added value of that land. He argued, for instance, that Leland Stanford and the Central Pacific Railroad should not be the sole beneficiary of the increase in the value of the property due to the construction of that railroad. George believed that the income derived from that tax then should be used for the benefit of the society. But not for the entire society, for George argued that the funds should only be distributed to White Americans. Chinese immigrants were not real Americans in his estimation. So although he was a visionary of more economic equality, George scapegoated the Chinese as vehemently as other American intellectuals. He in fact was a leader in the movement calling for Chinese exclusion. He saw the Chinese as the lackeys of the monopolist capitalists. In the economic crisis of the late nineteenth century, the Chinese were vilified by all sides.

The end of the nineteenth century was also a period of profound cultural crisis. The frontier had come to an end. Nineteenth century America had drawn its energies, its buoyancy, from the seemingly endless potential offered by an open frontier. So Turner was pondering, as an historian looking backward, but also peering forward, what would happen to a frontierless America.

Today, a century later, we are also experiencing a cultural crisis. This crisis is actually more complicated than that of an earlier century. Our cultural crisis manifests itself most significantly within two arenas. The first arena is our expanding racial diversity. Some time in the twenty-first century Whites will become a minority of the total U.S. population. In other words, the faces of America are changing. Already you can see the changing faces in every major city in the United States — San Francisco, Cleveland, Chicago, New York, Philadelphia, Washington, San Antonio, Los Angeles. And the question many people are asking is this: How will we define who is an American in the twenty-first century?

Fukuyama more dramatically addresses the second arena of our cultural crisis. Ever since the waning moments of World War II, the Cold War allowed us to discern our manifest destiny. America's manifest destiny was to contain communism. That would be the new frontier: the containment of communism — Vietnam, Cambodia, Laos, Cuba, Chile, Nicaragua, El Salvador, Guatemala. And now that the Soviet Union has collapsed and the Cold War is over, Francis Fukuyama encourages us to place our faith in liberal democracy and capitalism as guides to a brighter future. "History has ended."

Fukuyama's optimism is reflected in the way he ends his book, *The End of History*. He concludes with a story about a wagon train traveling west:

> Mankind will seem like a long wagon train, strung out along the road. Several wagons attacked by Indians will have been set aflame and abandoned along the way. There will be a few wagoneers who, stunned by the battle, will have lost their sense of direction and are temporarily heading in the wrong direction, but the great majority of wagons will be making the journey into town and most will eventually arrive there.

Here we have embedded in Fukuyama's final story a remarkable rendition of Turner's frontier thesis. Fukuyama intends his story about the wagon train moving west to illustrate his central thesis: All along "there had been only one journey and one destination."

Yet the very metaphor that Fukuyama has chosen raises more questions than it resolves: "whose" journey, "whose" destination, and "who" are "we?" Certainly, a good citizen should be able to embrace the larger narrative of what America is, the collective memory of who we are as a nation. But a good citizen must also be able to look "in a different mirror" and see the diversity that Americans reflect, to accept that we come with different faces and different names, like Garcia and Takaki. We are all American, and we should not have to explain or defend our citizenship every time we jump into a taxi cab. To draw from Walt Whitman's wonderful poetry, we must all become listeners — "to hear the varied carols of America," the songs and stories of our democratic diversity.

As we approach the coming multicultural millennium, we have to remind Fukuyama and his agreeing readers of William Faulkner's insight: "The past is not even past." Indeed, history has not ended. Rather it is sedimented into our present and our future. This powerful continuance of events and developments in our history requires us to know that history inclusively and accurately. This study of the past can enable us to confront the history of the enslavement of African Americans, the dispossession of Native Americans, the exploitation of Chinese immigrant workers, and the disciplining of Irish immigrant laborers. This understanding of our history can also guide toward a future where we might be able to work it out and get along in our diversity. After all, how many nations in the world have been founded, "dedicated," to use Lincoln's language, to the "proposition" that "all men are created equal"?

SEVEN

Latina/o Identity Politics

★   ★   ★

Linda Martín Alcoff

"OK by me in America!"
"For a small fee in America"
—*West Side Story*

In one of my classes some time back, during a group discussion of identity, a young Puerto Rican woman from New York City insisted against the disagreement of her classmates that she was an "American." She didn't want to be called Puerto Rican; she thought of herself simply as an "American." Knee-jerk leftist responses, mine included, have long treated such pronouncements as a species of false consciousness or ideological conditioning. Puertorriqueñas in this country are never considered simply "Americans" by Anglos, and to identify as such has seemed a naive position that will make one less prepared for racism. Moreover, identifying as American might be an indication of one's own internalized racism or great nation chauvinism.

But after this particular class, for some reason, I left dissatisfied and troubled by our routine critique of the professed desire to be seen simply as an "American." I began to try to think about her claim differently, to see what must be presupposed in her ability to make the claim, and to consider its political possibilities. This paper is my attempt to work out what these possibilities might mean.

★   ★   ★

The question of citizenship for U.S. Latinos is fraught with tensions that are in some respects different than for any other ethnic group. We are persistently seen by Anglo America as perennial foreigners: unassimilated, inassimilable, even uninterested in assimilation. Unlike other immigrant groups, our countries of origin are too close, our numbers here too numerous and concentrated, to motivate the loss of Spanish language or cultural custom.[1] Even though we may have lived in North America for generations, even if as Chicanos our families have never lived anywhere else, we are perceived as a foreign peoples squatting within the United States. This has prompted two sorts of responses. One is to reject those who have rejected us and to seek a life of dignity within a safe enclave, to turn the ghetto into a barrio where a communal life can flourish. The other response strives to make peace with the hegemonic Anglo society and learn to master its ways. This sometimes requires proving our loyalty by landing with the Marines in Panama City or infiltrating the parallel market in Los Angeles. But in both cases we have been pushed to choose, one or the other, a Latino life on the margins, or an Anglicized participant in the life of the nation.

This is beginning to change. Latinas/os have just in this generation become visible in the mainstream media even without changing their name and hiding their accent, as symbolized by the father-son stars Martin Sheen and Emilio Estevez. We are holding public office, hosting national radio shows, appearing on the nightly news as reporters and commentators and not just victims or perpetrators, and getting tenure in research universities. Latinas/os have made it into public culture, albeit still in small, unproportional numbers. The emergence of a Latina/o middle class creates the conditions both for more class collaboration and treachery as well as a better negotiating position with dominant Anglo institutions. And thus new worries emerge: Will the new pan-Latin identity lead eventually to Anglo assimilation once again, as our substantive and specific national identities are subsumed in an identity that only makes sense from the perspective of the Anglo-Latino divide? Will the price of entry into public culture be a loss of cultural integrity? Or will it bring to realization the hope expressed by

Guillermo Gómez-Peña that Latinos in the United States can some day "participate actively in a humanistic, pluralistic and politicized dialogue, continuous and not sporadic, and that this [will] occur between equals that enjoy the same power of negotiation"?[2]

Before Gómez-Peña's hope can be realized, however, I believe that "public intellectuals" in the United States need to rethink their understanding of the politics of identity in their dominant discourses and conversations. Both liberals and leftists are squeamish about identity politics, precisely out of a fear that emphasizing and politicizing identity gets in the way of creating progressive models of citizenship in which political judgment and the possibility of coalition should be based on one's views and commitments rather than one's background. In this paper I hope to cast some doubt on this truism.

(Particular) Identities/(Universalist) Politics

Identity politics is today attacked by right, left, and center. Todd Gitlin, the well known and widely published white leftist, provides a representative critique. In his view,

> . . . identity politics makes a fetish of the virtues of the minority, which, in the end, is not only intellectually stultifying but also politically suicidal. It creates a kind of parochialism in which one is justified in having every interest in difference and no interest in commonality . . . As soon as I declare I am a Jew, a black, a Hispanic, a woman, a gay, I have no more need to define my point of view.[3]

For Gitlin, identity politics distort, mislead, and generally thwart the development of a progressive political majority. The focus on identity directs us away from the class and economic issues by which we might build a unified, progressive agenda.

Interestingly, identity politics has also been rejected both by postmodernists and by liberals (which we should remember are not mutually exclusive categories) and is increasingly discredited within academic Anglo feminism. Postmodernism[4] has provided an influential critique of identities as dangerous fictions which efface difference and openendedness toward the aim of closure and absoluteness, and has also argued against reductionist or causal accounts of the relation between identity and politics (as if identities determine ones' politics), which would obscure the socially constructed character of identities as well as the socially constructed nature of the experiences that identities are often thought to be based upon. Many feminists have believed that a postmodern deconstruction of identity is the best way to respond to criticisms of the false universalism and overgeneralizations of White-dominated feminism.[5]

But another reason for rejecting identity politics is the general classical liberal ideology that understands the particularities of identity as less relevant to the political rights of persons than the universals of human *haecceity*. The great European revolutions of the modern period were articulated in universal terms for the rights of all, beyond differences of ancestry. This universalist language was a truly effective revolutionary stratagem against the feudal orders, in which identity determined one's life prospects without any chance for redress or alteration. The "rights of man" were counterposed to the rights of noblemen. By appealing to a universal human essence, revolutionaries could out trump feudal claims through the invocation of an underlying similarity between all men with more fundamental ethical and political importance than any differences of heritage or class identity.

This revolutionary discursive strategy of universalism has now become nearly hegemonic. Its use spread beyond class and heritage differences (i.e., nobility versus merchants) to other differences such as race and ethnicity. And thus the assumption that justice requires decreasing if not eliminating the social relevance of racial and ethnic particularity made its way into antiracist, integrationist movements in the United States. And the *political* value system of universalism over particularism was correlated with an *epistemological* value system where truth was defined as that which everyone can potentially know, as well as a *metaphysical* value system that derogated the particular to the universal. As Gary Peller has usefully pointed out:

> A commitment to a form of universalism, and an association of universalism with truth and particularism with ignorance, forms the infrastructure of American integrationist consciousness . . . Integrationist beliefs are organized around the familiar enlightenment story of progress consisting of the movement from mere belief and superstition to knowledge and reason, from the particular and therefore parochial to the universal and therefore enlightened.[6]

Where truth and justice are assumed to require universalism, cultural, racial, or ethnic identity cannot be accorded political significance without endangering progress.

It is in this ideological arena, which has heavily informed both the bourgeois mainstream thinking as well as the civil rights and social justice movements in the United States, which Latinos and Latinas are now entering as a recognized force. The apparently obvious need to make demands in the name of a universal is still a profound influence on both the left and the right, castigating specific demands to the derogatory realm of "special interests." Many are today concerned like Gitlin that U.S. multiculturalism is a form of tribalism that will produce a "homegrown Yugoslavia" if we continue to promote ethnic studies and divisive thinking on our college campuses.[7] Citizenship requires an investment in shared political institutions that identity politics defines as collaboration. And as a young white Anglo women's studies major explained to me at a talk I gave in Binghamton, New York recently, identity politics keeps people apart, it keeps people from seeing our similarities, and thus it keeps us from being able to become an effective political force.

I politely disagreed with this young woman. The acknowledgment and understanding of existing differences strengthens the likelihood of effective alliances. And having the effective possibility of separation can improve the quality of a relationship. Consider the analogy with divorce. Marriages in which divorce is illegal or virtually impossible usually suffer: The weaker partner cannot negotiate effectively when they have no practical means to leave the marriage. The possibility of divorce, even if one never takes advantage of it, can improve the quality of a relationship by ensuring that people are there because they want to be, not because they have no recourse. The right of self-determination, as the African American communist Harry Haywood argued years ago, operates in the same way. If minorities in this country have no recourse to autonomy, their conditions within the majority white society are unlikely to improve. Thus, sometimes that which might seem to pull us apart, such as the right to separate or the insistence on differences, actually works to improve the quality and strength of our connection.

Moreover, I suspect that the anxiety about separate identities is also motivated by this denigration of the particular realm vis-à-vis the universal. The philosophical idea that only the universal realm has truth and that the realm of the particular and the specific has validity or importance only to the extent that it can be subsumed within a universal theory, is an idea as old as Socrates and as wrong-headed as the idealization of the Greek polis. I would agree with Kierkegaard that actually the reverse is true: Any concept of the universal only has significance and truth to the extent that it is true for some particular "me," that is, to the extent that it can relate to my own, individual, particular existence, or to someone else's. Material reality is lived in the concreteness of particular lives, particular places, moments, and struggles. Universals are at times convenient but always inaccurate abstractions from concrete reality, and the criterion of their validity must always rest with the quality of their relation with the particular.

I would even agree with Judith Butler (and Hegel) that the *ontological* status of the universal subsists entirely in its particularist manifestation. As she explains:

> what one means by 'the universal' will vary, and the cultural articulation of that term in its various modalities will work against precisely the trans-cultural status of the claim. This is not to say that there ought to be no reference to the universal or that it has become, for us, an impossibility. On the contrary. All this means is that there are cultural conditions for articula-

tion which are not always the same, and that the term gains its meaning for us precisely through the decidedly less-than-universal cultural conditions of its articulation.[8]

But I don't really want to get into a philosophical argument here about the universal versus the particular. My point is that the evaluation of identity politics (and of multiculturalism and "special interests") has been stymied by assumptions that an emphasis on identity will fracture the body politic, this despite the fact that the critiques of identity politics are in some respects coming from opposite directions. Liberalism's aim is to achieve universality through emphasizing commonality, while postmodernism's goal is to acknowledge difference and avoid the totalitarian effects of closure by refusing identity. However, both sides unite in rejecting the political salience of *group identity*.[9]

This has produced an impasse between those who demand that we only make claims in terms of some universal, minimal but common notion of personhood and others of us who react to these demands with understandable insistence on the necessity of recognizing and even validating our plentiful differences. I believe that there is a way to move beyond this impasse between universality and the reactive insistence on difference as it manifests itself among progressive thinkers and activists in the United States today, and I also believe that what Latinas/os can in particular bring to this debate may be key in forging a new position.

Before I sketch this out, it will be helpful to compare the position Coco Fusco develops in her collection of essays, *English Is Broken Here*. Fusco is an artist but often writes art criticism on Latina/o art, which sometimes puts her in the uncomfortable position of presenting and translating an exotic "Otherness" for Anglo consumption. In the face of this, Fusco has endeavored to reposition herself "from being a 'minority' critic dutifully explaining Otherness to one who addresses whites as agents in an ongoing dynamic of racialization."[10] She wants to reposition the "Latina critic and Latina artist" from the margin to the center, from the observed to the observer, and through this reveal

what is observable from this location, which is a process of racial identity construction that ranges over Latina/o art but that is not produced
by Latina/o artists themselves. Thus Fusco makes two apparently contradictory points: The first is that Latino artists often include refer-
ences to their particular historical experiences in their works, but the
second is that the racialization of Latina/o art is produced not by Latinos themselves but by white Anglo consumers of "ethnic art." Her argument is that there is a disjuncture between what one might call the
self-conscious particularity of a lot of Latino art — its overt reference
to cultural history and experience — and the way in which this has
been taken up and interpreted in many Anglo art contexts as marking
and classifying the work as "ethnic art" and thus segregating it from
most European art which is simply classified as "art." The classification
of Latina/o art as ethnic art is not caused by features of the art so
much as it is by classification processes in the mainstream art world,
but Fusco develops this argument without it relying on an ability to
prove that Latina/o art is mostly trans-ethnic. Thus she has successfully
resisted framing the debate over Latina/o art in terms of "universality
versus difference" and suggested instead that there is a clash of what
we might think of as particular universals, that is, ways of thinking
about what art is.

Following this, Fusco argues that what is fundamentally at stake for
Latina/o artists is not so much "artistic freedom" (i.e., the freedom to
make ethnic art or political art) but "power — the power to choose,
the power to determine value" and the power to "change and redefine
one's identity."[11] In other words, the problem is not that Latina/o
artists produce ethnic art that then must be championed by liberal Anglos under the banner of artistic freedom, but that the very definition
and characterization of their art and of what art is and can be must be
opened to contestation rather than blindly based on Eurocentric interpretive traditions. Using Fusco's argument, I want to claim that the
aim of Latina/o identity politics is not simply greater visibility, a goal
that so stated will most likely result in increasing the commodification
of Latinas/os, but rather to make visible those processes that perpetu-
ate our marginalization and disempowerment. The ultimate struggle
is thus not simply to become visible (though this is a necessary part of

the goal), but to have power over the interpretive schemas that structure mainstream social practices of perception.

In some ways this formulation shares elements of a postmodernist framework, in emphasizing the processes by which representation occurs rather than simply attaining political rights for an already represented group, but I want to stress here that recognizing the political nature of processes of identity construction does not preclude the articulation of group identity or its political salience. Against those who would argue that any group categories oppress the individuals subsumed within them, I would argue that group-related differences and cultural and historical traditions are necessary to make sense of individual experience, to create narratives of the self that are vital for maximal agency and autonomy.[12] Sometimes what is shared most sharply are the very differences one has from the dominant cultural/political group, and those differences will be politically important in correlation to the extent the dominant group enjoys hegemony. The issue of noticing who has the power to represent is important not simply in order to resist any and all representations but in order to participate in the formulation of less reductive, less overly homogeneous, and more complex and adequate concepts of specific group identities.

Can We Learn From Latin America?

The political legacy of universalism is related to a particular European discourse of anti-aristocratic revolutionary struggle which, at the least, we should not automatically assume without argument is applicable to every political struggle. Moreover, as so many have shown, that universalist legacy was a false universalism exclusive of many constituencies, and thus the very pretension to universality made it difficult for these constituencies to reveal the exclusivist and particularist reality that the universalist discourses concealed. As a result, we have experienced a cultural period in which it was crucial to reveal specific differences and the particularities of identity. I want to turn now to the question of how we can move beyond this impasse between universalism and the insistence on difference.

To begin with, it is instructive to note that the great Latin American revolutions and liberation movements of the nineteenth and twentieth centuries were by and large not couched in universalist terms. The figure known as "The Liberator" of Latin America, Venezuelan Simón Bolívar, originally raised the demand for political self-determination as a right based on a specific identity. Europeans had justified their colonization of Latin America on the basis of claims about the Native peoples, as well as their mestizo offspring, claims in which indigenous peoples were characterized as sub-human and uncivilized and therefore incapable and unworthy of political autonomy. European intellectuals considered Latin America a bastard culture, without coherent traditions, and thus doomed to cultural impotence. They believed that racial hybridity led to decreased fertility and diminished health, and that race-mixing would degrade the "superior" race without comparably uplifting the "inferior" race.[13]

In response to this, the anticolonial discourse in Latin Americans made counterclaims concerning the character of Latin American identity and the fruitfulness precisely of our heterogny. José Carlos Mariátegui, the Peruvian Marxist, created an original vision of a new society that would be based not only on socialist principles but also on "an Indo-Hispanic cultural legacy."[14] Like Mao Zedong, Mariátegui freely transformed European-based socialist thought to a Peruvian context with its own, agrarian-based, culturally specific form of indigenous communitarianism. José Vasconcelos, Mexican politician and author of *The Cosmic Race*, created a vision of intercontinental liberation that would be based on a newly emerging mestizo identity, claiming mestizos as the new vanguard population that could usher in political liberation for all. And the Mexican revolution itself, arguably the most important revolution of this hemisphere, articulated its mandate in racial and ethnic identity terms, not as an alliance of peasants and workers, but an alliance of Indians and mestizos. Some of these invocations of identity, of course, involved antiblack and anti-indigenous racisms. Vasconcelos' in particular had strong elements of anti-black racism and his valorization of mestizos was made in comparative terms as against black identity. But this fact does not prove that *any* discourse of identity will be racist or that it will exclude persons who should not be excluded. Before we peremptorily reject this different tradition of political discourse, there are important lessons to be drawn from it.

First, this tradition more readily recognizes that identities are developed historically and often in connection with political discourses and political claims. Linguistic conceptualizations of identity can directly affect the material reality of people's lives, their self-understanding and social practices, and the distribution of political and economic power. Revolutions that invoked mestizo peoples as central representatives of the nation, which valorized mestizo peoples against slavish European mimicry, but also put mestizo peoples above Afro-Latin and indigenous people as more central to the nation, had material, political effects and were self-conscious political strategies. In this discursive tradition, recognizing that identities were being socially constructed and that they were operating within historical contexts to advance strategic aims did not mean that identities were viewed as simple opportunist strategies or total illusions having no purchase on lived experience. In order to be taken up and have real effect, identity discourses must resonate with at least some of the contradictory truths of everyday reality. But Latin American theorists were concerned not merely to make identities visible, but to help form and shape identities as part of a decolonizing psychological process and political movement.[15]

Secondly, we can note that within Latin America, the developing discourse of identity, and in particular, the discourse of mestizo identity, has been from its inception intrinsically connected to a discourse of nationalism and of the right to national sovereignty and self-determination. In the face of a European aggressor who espoused universalist rhetoric, the most effective opposing rhetoric would not be one that replicated universalist pretensions, but one that asserted rights from within a specified identity. The result was that in much of Latin America what Lyotard calls legitimation narratives, or narratives that legitimated the current political institutions that made up the state, were grounded on identity narratives. Thus, an attentiveness to the specificity of Latin American identity, as against universal abstractions like "man," were not viewed as leading to Balkanization or a breakdown of the state or the society, but precisely as necessary for the consolidation of the society and its ability and right to demand sovereignty. Thus, identity narratives were necessary conditions *before* citizenship could be practiced or even contemplated.

Third, the history of identity discourse in Latin America used against universalist discourses from Europe reveals the often unacknowledged interdependence of identity concepts. The construction of a concept of Latin American identity did not develop in isolation, based entirely on "internal" features. It was constructed in an oppositional relationship to Spain, Portugal, and other forces of colonization. The very arguments that Vasconcelos made to champion mestizo identity were made in comparative terms, that the internal heterogeneity of the mestizo peoples was superior to the homogeneity of the Europeans and Anglo-Americans.

Interestingly, this also meant that the argument for mestizo value became dependent on a suppression or deemphasis of Anglo-European heterogeneity. After all, it was only through the experience of conquest, through the mediation of the "New World," that Europe started thinking of itself as Europe rather than a collection of warring monarchies with different languages and different cultural traditions. And of course, it was also the case that the Anglo-European self-understanding as the highest civilization depended on its reflected contrast in cultures it labeled backward and barbarian. How could Europe portray its own history of constant internal warfare, its violent enforcement of social hierarchies, and the persistence of its monarchies as the paradigm of enlightenment? Only through its claims to a comparative superiority vis-à-vis the societies in the rest of the world. In this light, Winston Churchill's often quoted remark that democracy, though terrible, is better than any of its alternatives, can be reread as an implicit claim about the European polis that would go something like this: "Though often chaotic and violent, still thank God we are Europeans and not Africans, Asians, or Latin Americans!" Most importantly, the interdependence of identity reveals the real source of resistance to demands for Latin American rights and sovereignty: if the colonized countries can claim to be great and progressive civilizations, the status of Europe's own civilization must come into question.

Identity Discourses in the United States

Although U.S. political discourse espoused universalism, there has also existed alongside this a strategy of exclusion and discrimination based on an identity discourse of Nativism, which based economic and political rights on claims of longevity and stories of origin. Nativist claims base a concept of U.S. identity (commonly understood in North America as being "American") on long-established tenure, on being here before the Revolution, and on contributing to the formation of the culture. These are the criteria of demarcation between "real Americans" and "foreigners." On this basis, it is argued that recent Latina/o immigrants, whether legal or illegal, have less claim than others to political and economic rights. One commonly hears statements of resentment toward Latinas/os getting jobs who "don't even speak English," as Derrick Bell has his figure Jesse B. Semple put it.[16] Increasingly, all Latina/os, whether U.S. citizen or not, are being subjected to searches and interrogations at the border, demands for proof of citizenship not requested from others, and in some cases refused employment.[17]

Nativist discourse targets not only those who are considered unassimilated but also those considered inassimilable. White European immigrants such as Poles and Russians may have come more recently than others, but many people in the United States view them as more readily assimilable than immigrants from the Caribbean or Central and South America. Part of the reasoning here is racial, but language and cultural differences are also considered crucial. European immigrants are far from home and less likely to retain their language after the first generation. The similarities between their cultural traditions and dominant U.S. traditions are also thought to lead to easy assimilation. Asians, on the other hand, are considered "too different," and the proximity of a Spanish speaking homeland reduces the motivation for U.S. Latina/os to adopt English as one's primary or even unique language. This criteria — involving the ability and motivation to assimilate — explains why even Chicanos are considered beyond the pale of interpellated "Americanness." If anyone could claim "Nativism,"

Mexicans who live north of the U.S.-Mexico border could claim it, of course. But by the criterion of assimilability, even Chicanos are treated as non-Native; they live here in spirit only, but are not part of the U.S. cultural identity.

Nuestra América

All of these concepts (Nativism, assimilability, racism) are strategies of exclusion based on sometimes implicit, sometimes explicit invocations of an American (meaning U.S.) *identity,* which has specific, particular attributes (White, or "Native," or Europeanized). Thus, what is interesting to notice about these various anti-immigrant arguments is that they amount to an identity discourse, a narrative of the polis fully dependent on and integrated with a specific cultural character and ethnic combination (sometimes including only whiteness and sometimes extending somewhat beyond whiteness). The paradox for Newt Gingrich and William Bennett is that what makes "Western values" superior is their (supposed) transcendent universal applicability, but what makes Western values possible is, as Peter Brimelow, Allan Bloom, and Pat Buchanan candidly argue, the maintenance of racial exclusiveness and cultural hierarchies. In other words, this country is superior to all others because it promotes tolerance and freedom for all, but it can only continue to promote these if we keep European-Americans in the majority and in political and cultural dominance over all others. This point of view reveals that, despite the opening of the Declaration of Independence and the pretensions of universalism, this country (like so many others) is founded on a substantive cultural and racial conception of what a specific U.S. identity is.

If this is right, and discrimination in the United States is justified ultimately not on a claim about American universalism but a claim about American specificity, then it may seem as if only a universal discourse about human rights and individuality can be an effective counter. On this view, multiculturalism and identity politics are in the long run, regardless of the intentions of their proponents, an obstacle to the true expansion of democracy, because they highlight the ways in which some U.S. constituencies are different from the paradigm of

Americanness and therefore less capable of the investments required of citizenship. Moreover, it might be argued that identity discourses exacerbate those differences by promoting the maintenance rather than the withering away of difference. On this view, rather than promoting specific identities, we should be striving to lessen the political importance of identity through universalism.

I want to suggest that it might be more fruitful to think about this in a different way. The point of noticing that identity discourses are central to U.S. political discourse is that the United States is not, therefore, so unlike Latin America as it assumes. Its dominant legitimation narratives are about cultural identity, not anonymous individuality. Moreover, I would suggest that the particular conception of U.S. identity that has been dominant (not that there is a single, internally coherent one but more like a cluster) is also in some respects more like those in Latin America than in Europe. Latin American nations were founded out of a colonial history, initially in an anticolonial revolt, as was the U.S. Latin American nations were also from the beginning conglomerations of cultural, ethnic, and racial differences, as was the United States. An honest appraisal of U.S. identity would come to realize the way in which the similarity between the United States and the rest of the hemisphere has been suppressed. The United States is not a mono-racial, essentially European nation. Less and less is it an economic superpower, and thus less and less can it afford to maintain its status as a military superpower. Rather, the United States, like Canada, Mexico, and Brazil, must worry about attracting capital, must give non-U.S. based multinationals tax breaks to lure them here, and must be wary of having more capital-rich countries like Germany and Japan take advantage of it. This lesson in humility is of course, from my point of view, all to the good.

I am not suggesting that the United States of America will quietly and happily slip into more egalitarian relations with its hemispheric neighbors, and through this come to accept its own internal Latina/o populations as full political players and cultural insiders. I agree with Richard Rodriguez's claim that the so-called celebration of hispano culture going on in the United States is in actuality, as he puts it, because "America wants to eat Mexico." But I do believe that the economic decline could motivate some moves in this direction, and that toward promoting this it is in our interest to encourage a new debate over U.S. identity, what it consists of, and what it means.

Given the similarities that actually exist throughout this hemisphere, and given the implicit identity narratives already at play in the United States, my suggestion, in short, is that rather than attempting to salvage an anonymous universalism, we need a new debate over the terms and constitution of a substantive U.S. cultural identity. What is needed is a national debate over the *specificity* of U.S. identity, one that will be able to explicitly address covert claims to Nativism and assimilability as well as racism. Such a project does not require us to de-emphasize identity and difference but to formulate a heterogeneous and inclusive cultural identity that incorporates our specific ethnic traditions. The choice is not between Latina/o identity versus a generic Americanness with no substantive content other than political platitudes, but rather to understand how we can choose both Latina/o identity and a larger substantive identity for all who live in the United States. To be an "American," or, as I would prefer, an *estadounidense,* is to be located in a country with a specific history, a history of paradoxical political valence and continuous negotiations between diverse cultural practices and values, a country that was capable of producing but incapable of embracing a James Baldwin, a country in which a world-inspiring movement for civil rights was both made necessary and made possible. To be an estadounidense is to be a person whose tastes in food, clothing, favorite slang words, and preferred music has been profoundly affected by Latino, European and African, Asian and indigenous, traditions even when we are unaware of the influence. I don't have the time or space here to provide more conjecture on what a newly configured American identity might contain, but it seems clear that its racial associations, historical teleologies, and global allegiances need to be radically transformed.

In the United States today, 73.6 percent of Latinas/os identify as Latina/o first, American second.[18] Strengthening our participation in U.S. political culture does not require changing this identification. However, it does require a revised understanding of how Latinas/os relate to an "American" identity. We who are Latina/os need to begin to think of ourselves — and understand ourselves — as cultural insiders rather than cultural outsiders, as longstanding contributors to the essence of "Americanness," and as full players in formulating a new national consciousness rather than restricted to defending our embattled communities.

Thus, what I am suggesting is that Latina/o identity politics should be raised to the national level and understood as central to an ongoing discourse over national identity. It is a mistake to assume that Latina/o identity politics is sequestered to the realm of the particular. By suggesting it move to the national realm, I am not suggesting it aspire to universalism, but that it can contribute to the development of a new *concrete* (and thus particular formulation of the) universal. Such a concept does not simply side with difference against universality or vice versa, but attempts a reconfiguration.

As Baldwin argued many years ago, the struggle for citizenship requires teaching minority children to feel an ownership toward this country, a sense, not that they belong to it, but that it, in all its beauty and terror, *belongs to them*.[19] This will prove to be, perhaps, the most powerful resistance strategy of all. Ann Laura Stoler has explored such a resistance strategy that was used against French and Dutch colonial powers by women in Indochina, Madagascar, and the Indies in the late nineteenth century, in which

> children of "mixed-blood" or even of "purely native origin" were acknowledged by European men who were supposedly not their natural fathers. These claims to paternity, in which a European man of modest or impoverished means would allegedly be paid a fee by a native woman to recognize her child, could redefine who "by descent" was European and who was not . . . . [Thus] these were racial reorderings outside the state's control.[20]

Colonial authorities were very threatened by what they called these "fraudulent recognitions," worrying that they would be "submerged by a flood of naturalized natives" by this introduction into their midst of a "questionable population."[21] My suggestion is that a similar effect of resistance may be produced when there is a cultural appropriation of "American" identity by young Puertorriqueños in New York. They are claiming rights to a patrimony most consider beyond their reach. Perhaps they will help us to refashion an American identity beyond no one's reach.[22]

Notes

1. See Juan Flores and George Yudice, "Living Borders/Buscando América: Languages of Latino Self-Formation" in *Social Text* 24 (1990): 57-84; see also Suzanne Oboler, *Ethnic Labels, Latino Lives: Identity and the Politics of (Re)Presentation in the United States* (Minneapolis: University of Minnesota Press, 1995).

2. Guillermo Gómez-Peña, "Documented/Undocumented," in *The Graywolf Annual Five: Multicultural Literacy* eds. Rick Simonson and Scott Walker (Saint Paul, Minn.: Graywolf Press, 1988), 133.

3. Todd Gitlin, "On the Virtues of a Loose Canon" in *Beyond PC: Towards a Politics of Understanding* ed. Patricia Aufderheide (Saint Paul, Minn.: Graywolf Press, 1992), 188. See also his full-scale attack on identity politics in *The Twilight of Common Dreams: Why America is Wracked by Culture Wars* (New York: Henry Holt and Co., 1995).

4. I recognize that this term tends to simplify and homogenize a very complex field of texts. All of what goes by the name "postmodernism" will not be subject to the descriptions I give in what follows. Nonetheless, it remains a useful shorthand.

5. For this argument, see, e.g., Nancy Fraser and Linda Nicholson, "Social Criticism without Philosophy: An Encounter between Feminism and Postmodernism," in *Feminism/Postmodernism* ed. Linda Nicholson (New York: Routledge, 1990), 19–38. For the counter argument, see Susan Strickland, "Feminism, Postmodernism,and Difference," in *Knowing the Difference: Feminist Perspectives in Epistemology* eds. Kathleen Lennon and Margaret Whitford (London: Routledge, 1994), 265–74.

6. Gary Peller, "Race Consciousness" in *After Identity: A Reader in Law and Culture* eds. Danielson and Karen Engle (New York: Routledge, 1995), 74.

7. Gitlin, "On the Virtues of a Loose Cannon," 190.

8. Judith Butler, "For a Careful Reading" in *Feminist Contentions* eds. Benhabib, et al. (New York: Routledge, 1995).

9. On this latter point, see J. L. A. Garcia, "Affirmative Action and Hispanic Americans," *APA Proceedings* vol. 68, no. 5 (May 1995):139–42; see also Leon Wieseltier, "Against Identity," *New Republic* 28 Nov. 1994, 24–32.

10. Coco Fusco, *English is Broken Here: Notes on Cultural Fusion in the Americas* (New York: The New Press, 1995), 68.

11. Ibid.

12. In support of this point there are useful arguments in Satya Mohanty, *Literary Theory and the Claims of History: Postmodernism, Objectivity, Multicultural Politics* (Ithaca, N.Y.: Cornell University Press, 1997); and in Lorraine Code, *Rhetorical Spaces: Essays on Gendered Locations* (New York: Routledge, 1995); and in Diana Tietjens Meyers, *Feminists Rethink the Self* (Boulder, Colo.: Westview Press, 1997).

13. See e.g., Walter Mignolo, *The Darker Side of the Renaissance: Literacy, Territoriality, and Colonization* (Ann Arbor, Mich.: University of Michigan Press, 1995); Miquel Leon-Portilla, ed., *The Broken Spears: The Aztec Account of the Conquest of Mexico* (Boston: Beacon Press, 1992); Sandra Harding, ed., *The "Racial" Economy of Science* (Bloomington, Ind.: Indiana University Press, 1993); Robert Young *Colonial Desire: Hybridity in Theory, Culture, and Race* (New York: Routledge, 1995); Emmanuel Eze, ed., *Race and the Enlightenment* (Cambridge, Mass.: Blackwell, 1997); Stephen Greenblatt, ed., *New World Encounters* (Berkeley: University of California Press, 1993); José Rabasa, *Inventing A-M-E-R-I-C-A: Spanish Historiography and the Formation of Eurocentrism* (Norman, Okla.: University of Oklahoma Press, 1993).

14. See José Carlos Mariátegui, *Seven Interpretative Essays on Peruvian Reality,* trans. Marjory Urguidi (Austin, TX: University of Texas Press, 1971) and Ofelia Schutte, *Cultural Identity and Social Liberation in Latin American Thought* (Albany, N.Y.: SUNY Press, 1993), esp. chap. 2.

15. One of the clearest examples of this approach is in Samuel Ramos, *Profile of Man and Culture in Mexico*, trans. Peter G. Earle (Austin, TX: University of Texas Press, 1962). See also Frantz Fanon, *Black Skin/White Masks*, trans. Charles Lam Markman (New York: Grove Press, 1965).

16. Derrick Bell, *Faces at the Bottom of the Well: The Permanence of Racism* (New York: Basic Books, 1992), 24.

17. See Leslie Marmon Silko, "Fences Against Freedom," in *Hungry Mind Review* 31 (Fall 1994): 9–59.

18. *Harper's Magazine* (April 1996) 60.

19. James Baldwin, "A Talk to Teachers," in *The Graywolf Annual Five,* p. 3–12.

20. Ann Laura Stoler, *Race and the Education of Desire: Foucault's History of Sexuality and the Colonial Order of Things* (Durham, N.C.: Duke University Press, 1995), 48–9; see also her "Sexual Affronts and Racial Frontiers: European Identities and the Cultural Politics of Exclusion in Colonial Southeast Asia," *Comparative Studies in Society and History* 34.2 (July 1992): 514–51.

21. Raoul Abor, *Des Reconnaissance Frauduleuses d'Enfants Naturels en Indochine* (Hanoi: Imprimerie Tonkinoise, 1917), 41; Quoted in Stoler, *Race and the Education of Desire,* 49.

22. I would like to thank the following people for extremely helpful comments and criticisms of an earlier draft of this paper: Paula Moya, Arlene Davila, Karin Rosemblatt, Eduardo Mendieta, and Caroline Tauxe.

EIGHT

Becoming Citizens,
Becoming Hispanics[1]

★   ★   ★

Eduardo Mendieta

There is no more central institution to democracy than that of citizenship. A government of the people, by the people, for the people is meaningless without this mechanism that empowers and enables human beings to assume the charge, responsibility, and right to rule themselves as a community. Without citizens, there is no democracy. But just as democracy has been the accomplishment of social and political movements, citizenship has also been redefined by some of these same movements. In fact, many of the sociopolitical movements that through their struggles brought about greater democracy in American society were social movements that sought redefinitions of American citizenship. American citizenship has evolved by having been made more inclusive and more expansive. In other words, citizenship has been made to apply to and subsume members of the community who were up to that point not recognized as civic partners and equals. Or, citizenship has been transformed, making it more expansive, and thus more inclusive and welcoming to persons who were not members of the civic community but participated, or could participate, in the national project in some fashion. In short, just as American democracy has a history, American citizenship also has a history. At times their histories have run parallel, but at other times they have been at odds. It is known, for instance, that while American democracy was born proclaiming the equality of all human beings, its citizenship was inaugurated with the exclusion not only of African slaves and women, but also of white males who owned no property. American citizenship, which was supposed to ensure the integrity of American democracy, has been racialized and sexualized since its inception, thus contradicting the fundamental tenant of American democracy that all human beings are born equal. This racialization and sexualization became so entrenched in American democratic thought and practice that it was only until the first half of the twentieth century that American citizenship began to be commensurate with the universal, liberal, and civic ideals proclaimed in the American Constitution and its amendments. In many ways one can even say that American democracy has been realized through the acquisition of citizenship by groups, peoples, races, and ethnicities that had previously been seen as both not worthy and not capable of participating in the self-legislation of the American body politic. American democracy has been the result of the struggles for citizenship by purported unworthy or problematic selves and subjects.

Today, as in the nineteenth century and the early part of the twentieth, American citizenship faces serious challenges. These challenges come both from without and within. From without, the challenges stem from the processes of globalization that are making us all citizens of one world. Globalization ought to be understood not solely in terms of greater economic integration and interdependence, but also as the cultural, political, and social creolization and hybridization of the planet. Globalization, thus, means that we have become vulnerable to risks assumed by others, and vice versa, but also that we have become co-producers of a world culture. One of the most important aspects of globalization, however, is the challenge to the hegemony and autonomy of the nation state, the means through which communities and nations affirm their right to self-legislation. This aspect of globalization, onerous to some but appealing to others, requires that we, as nominal citizens of one world, reach decisions together about matters that affect us all. Indeed, in our contemporary context we may even speak of a "global citizen." This topic, however, is the other half of this essay that cannot be presented.

From within, the challenges to American citizenship come from voter apathy, the disintegration of a common civic culture, the resurgence of nativism movements, and from the growing resentment and even hate of immigrants and foreigners who are seen as both threats and social leeches. The Reaganite neo-liberal economic revolution of de-regulation and Bush's attack on big government, coupled with close to two decades of recisionist economy, created a general feeling of fear and anxiety in the United States. Fear and anxiety are always fertile ground for xenophobia, jingoism, and nativism. And the attack on the welfare state, the reluctance to seriously consider a national healthcare program, the general skepticism and backlash against feminist ideals and goals, as well as the attack on affirmative action programs, as manifestation of this fear and anxiety, have corroded any notion of a common national ethos or calling. The fact is that while feminist, racial, ethnic and identity politics are faulted for the 'disuniting of America,' the real culprits are neo-liberal policies, the restructuring of the American economy, and the increasing ostracism and exclusion of greater numbers of American citizens. As we squat in the squalor of a public square, private affluence reaches unthought and unscalable heights. In such times, the "foreigner," whether real or imagined, becomes the target of our social intolerance and atavism.

Although it might seem otherwise, these two challenges to American citizenship are related. Globalization does not proceed one way. America is not the only agent of globalization, it is also globalized by other agents. One of the main ways in which American citizenship is challenged by these processes and pressures can be found in the claims for social justice made by immigrants and ethnic minorities within the United States. These immigrants are part and parcel of United States's history of colonial/imperial intervention, occupation, economic neo-colonization, and military vigilantism. Today, the United States has the largest immigrant population of any nation in the world. Immigrants amount to almost 10 percent of the total population. Of this percentage, the greatest number are Hispanics. In fact, it has been forecasted by many demographers and by the U.S. Census Bureau that by the turn of the next millennium, Hispanics will constitute the largest ethnic minority in the country, surpassing African Americans.

In the following, I hope to illuminate the issue of an evolving American citizenship and the immediate challenges it faces vis-á-vis immigrants and ethnic minorities in the United States. At the same time, I will look at Hispanics and explore the interconnected questions of cultural identity and political participation. But this investigation is no mere academic exercise. I hope that my analysis will result in making clear a dual challenge: one to American citizenship and another to Hispanics. At stake, it seems to me, is the future of American democracy in an age of greater ethnic diversity and global codependence.

Becoming Citizens

Citizenship first evolved, as T. H. Marshall noted almost fifty years ago, through a dual process of geographical fusion and functional separation.[2] Citizenship developed with the creation of nations, and later expanded with the transformation of nations into nation states.[3] It is for these reasons that citizenship is both a cultural status and a legal capacity. The contemporary nation state is often plagued by the inner paradox of including as members of the community only those individuals who form part of the imaginary community that constitutes the nation while at the same time declaring in its Constitution that it, as a legal state, counts as equals all its members, regardless of their social, cultural, racial, gender status. Analogously, citizenship is plagued by the internal contradiction that it must be seen simultaneously as both a cultural and social status and a legal capacity, a capacity which allows citizens to stand above any kind of social inequality.[4] We will see how this internal tension is compounded by conflicts in contemporary society. For the moment, let us note that this tension refers to the two modalities in which citizenship can be enacted or participated in by social agents: as an ascribed cultural and social status or as an inalienable legal capacity and entitlement.

One may speak of the elements or parts of citizenship, but also of ideal citizenship, of the way in which social agents can best live out their citizenship. The cogency and feasibility of ideal citizenship, or of model citizenship, is, however, predicated on both the differentiation and interconnection of the elements that constitute citizenship. Following Marshall and MacPherson, we can say that citizenship has as its central elements civil, political, and social rights.[5] Civil rights can be thought of as the neural column upon which the whole organic system of rights is predicated. Political rights are the muscles of the organism. And social rights are its nourishment and sheltering flesh, so to speak.

Civil rights are personal and individual. Sometimes they are said to be inalienable and thus to appear as part of natural law. They provide the rationale for the following: freedom of speech and publication, freedom of conscience and religion, freedom of association and movement, freedom from the arbitrary use of state force and from the impartial use of justice, freedom from invasion of one's privacy by either the state or other persons, and freedom to own private property, and thus, freedom to enter and execute valid contracts. In general, these are rights protecting against the state and against the illegitimate use of coercion whether political, legal, or physical.

Political rights are also personal rights, but they only acquire meaning or significance in the context of social relations. In other words, these rights acquire meaning only when used in concert with other citizens striving for similar political goals. Political rights include the right to participate in the development, acquisition, and delegation of political power. It is through political rights that civil rights become a power or force that can be enacted against the state, through the state.

Finally, social rights, which are of a more recent vintage in the unfolding of citizenship rights, are less rights of individuals than of groups. These rights, in other words, are not assumed to be equally valid for all, but only for some. In contrast to civil rights and political rights, furthermore, they are not rights against the state, but are rights granted, or enabled, by the state. They are thus dependent on the kinds of institutions that constitute the modern welfare nation state. Social rights constitute the following rights: to work, to a minimum wage, to education, to social security against involuntary unemployment and the social consequences of old age, illness, even the death of the head of a household. These rights even include rights to leisure and rest (paid vacations and holidays, for instance), to maternal and paternal leave, and even to bereavement. In short, social rights are rights to social services. Social rights consist of rights to a level of existence consistent with human dignity, and respect for the well-being of the whole person. Through these rights, a citizen is empowered to participate in the cultural, political, social, and institutional heritage of a nation.[6]

Citizenship, then, is made up of a neural system constituted by individual rights against the state; rights to participate in the state that constitutes a system of muscles that allows individuals to act in concert with others; and rights that are conditional upon the state, but that attend to the integral dignity of the person, and thus can be thought of as the flesh that shelters the neural and muscular systems. While each element may have evolved at different stages, more or less, in tandem with the evolution of the state, they nonetheless constitute a systematic and coherent whole. Many political theoreticians have noted that the unfolding of these elements that constitute citizenship corresponded to the English, American, and French revolutions, each more or less having inaugurated the next level of internal differentiation of rights pertaining to citizenship. This historical parallelism, however, must be accepted with great reservations. For, in the last instance, regardless of whether the English, the American, or French revolutions had taken place, civil rights inevitably would have demanded for political rights, which in turn would have required social rights. In Habermas's view, in fact, the unfolding of rights corresponds to an internal normative dynamic of both nation states and their concomitant citizenship. The point to be established here is that today we can see that while citizenship has evolved, its contemporary integrity and meaning hinges on the interconnection of all three sets of rights.[7]

It was already noted that citizenship is transformed by being made either more inclusive or more expansive. Existing rights are either extended to hitherto disenfranchised members of the community, or new rights are articulated and claimed that will address needs or conditions not covered by already existing rights. This distinction might turn out to be merely heuristic and analytic, for in practice, and as history has amply demonstrated, when members of a community are made civic equals, new rights are necessitated that will make possible their equal participation in all the other rights of the civic union.

Similarly, when new rights are 'discovered' for both new and old members of the community, these require that all pre-existing rights be equally accessible to the new citizens. A case in point is the Fourteenth Amendment, from which the whole fabric of rights against discrimination and equal participation in the benefits and duties of society stem. More concretely, from the Fourteeth Amendment there unfolded logically the rights not only against sexual discrimination, but also against discrimination because of a physical handicap, and discrimination based on sexual orientation. The important point to be foregrounded about this heuristic distinction is that the rights of citizens are contingent upon social movements. Whether citizenship rights are made to apply to new citizens, or new rights are discovered or pronounced, this all depends upon the efforts of groups that claim inclusion and argue for their own equal participation in the community. Now, social movements ought to be broadly understood to mean not just political and economic movements, but also cultural and even spiritual movements. It is because there have been social movements that have put pressure on the state, and the ruling opinion of the day, that citizenship has expanded and has been made more inclusive. Constitutional amendments have been the result as much of major changes in the structure of the nation, such as the Civil War, as of movements like the Woman Suffrage movement and the Civil Rights movement. Social movements, most importantly, have brought about a transformation of citizenship through the transformation of citizens themselves. Indeed, it is in the context of the new social movements that more expansive notions of citizenship were first forged. Social movements have been the crucible in which new citizens were created. It is later that these notions of a new citizen solidified, so to say, into the constitutional and legal codes of the body politic. If the law is a relay mechanism between the constitution of a nation and its moral character, as Habermas notes, social movements are the place where the moral insights of a political community are lived out, nurtured, and transformed into feasible citizenship rights.

Social movements, interestingly, are agents of transformation insofar as they raise, if not universalizable, at least generalizable claims within a society out of their own particular and unique experiences of deprivation, exclusion, and disenfranchisement. In other words, social movements translate their particular and unique experiences of privation and suffering into either universalizable or generalizable rights claims. Thus, for instance, the first social movement of all, the workers movement, transformed their social status of privation into a critique of the political status quo, thus bringing about the expansion of citizenship through the expansion of political rights. The worker, living in a situation of inequality, claimed political rights to associate, to enter into contract, to a fair trial, etc., so that his/her situation of inequality could be matched by a situation of civil and political equality. Yet the rights that workers claimed for themselves were rights that ought to have been extended to every member of the community. Conversely, subjects of the civic community that did not receive these rights would be thereby deprived of a full standing in this community and thus denied complete access to its benefits, rights, and duties. In short, a worker without rights came to be seen as no less than an indentured servant, and the individuals with complete access to the rights of the nation as no more than another aristocracy.

In her Tanner Lectures Judith Shklar brilliantly illustrated how the struggle for inclusion has been a struggle for rights that ought to be generalizable to all. She demonstrated how the shadow of slavery has darkened the history of American citizenship precisely insofar as those who have sought inclusion in the body politic by means of a transformation of its citizenship have always used the condition of the slave as the negation of the dignity of the person.[8] Thus, social movements within the United States have always referred to the slave as the negative condition that would result from either privation of the right to vote or the right to earn one's own living. Slavery is the absolute negation of all humanity, thus any movement that sought to depart from, or keep in abeyance any social structure that might lead to this condition made universalizable rights claims. In other words, no one ought to be treated as a slave and no one should submit to any situation in which she would be treated as though she were a slave. Women argued thus, although equivocally. At first, by suggesting that women would be no less than slaves if they were not enfranchised. Later, by suggesting that they could not be slaves because of their high moral standing and education, and thus their not being enfranchised was an affront to them. The condition of the slave was what no one should have been made to descend to and what everyone should have been protected from.

To this day, American citizenship has yet to disavow its deeply entrenched racism, which takes shape in its racialization of citizenship. It remains bewitched by the dark gaze of slavery. It should not be forgotten that "Asians" could not become citizens until the second half of this century, and that many a Mexican American, despite the Guadalupe Hidalgo Treaty of 1848, continued to be treated as second-class citizens until after World War II. Many other similar cases can be brought forth.[9] Nonetheless, the point I am trying to illustrate and establish is that social movements always begin from situations and conditions of political, economic, social, and cultural privation, isolation, exclusion, and suffering. These experiences are then translated into claims that are applicable to all. For, in short, an injustice to one is an injustice to all, and conversely, a right that only some have is but a privilege and thus not a real right. Rights are powers and entitlements that we all should be able to claim and have access to. It is, however, only individuals in social contexts who have insight into the rights that they both possess and might lack. As Linda Martín Alcoff noted with respect to her defense of identity politics, "any concept of the universal has significance and truth to the extent that it is true for some particular 'me,' that is, to the extent that it can relate to my own individual, particular existence, or to someone else's."[10] Rights, in short, only have meaning if they have signficance for a particular person or group. For they alone can test their validity and reach. This, in turn, has as its other side, or complement, the fact that social movements are made possible by citizenship rights even though they are contributing to the elucidation of such rights. As J. M. Barbalet put it: "Social movements contribute to and are facilitated by citizenship."[11] In other words, citizenship rights need and call forth social movements. A social movement is witness to an inchoate right or a right yet to be made explicit. A lack of social movements reveals the absence of citizenship rights. Social movements, in fact, are the lifeline of citizenship rights. On the other hand, a complete absence of citizenship rights can result in the birthing of social, political, and cultural movements for the right to have rights. In such cases, social movements become struggles for the social space in which citizens can be citizens.

It is this interdependence between social movements and citizenship rights, their mutuality in short, that is at issue when questions of cultural identity and political participation are raised. Social movements are ways of claiming cultural identity; that is, cultural identity is affirmed and forged through social movements. In contrast, political participation has often been construed as a process by means of which one disavows one's cultural uniqueness and social locality. This at least has been the way political participation and cultural identity have been related within the liberal tradition that has guided American political thought. Yet, as was noted above, political participation is an extension of one's cultural identity. Indeed, with Renato Rosaldo, we must speak of a "cultural citizenship," or a culture of citizenship.[12] Culture, the ways in which social agents construct their social space, determines their citizenship, while the enactment of citizenship in turn transforms and conditions one's culture. Social movements are a place where this codetermination is catalyzed.

Becoming Hispanic

Social labels, ethnic markers, and racial categories are no less arbitrary and no less fraught with power differentials than the lines that mark a map circumscribing a geopolitical unit. Like the boundaries that determine the limits of nations, ethnic and racial labels include as well as exclude. They are the result of the enactment of power by some over others. Yet there is a dynamic between being labeled and identifying oneself. One resists a label by naming oneself. By naming oneself, one might circumvent or disable and neutralize a label. Frontiers and borders are contested, and not just from the side of the colonizer. They remain ever porous sites of negotiation and even compromise. At times, similarly ethnic and racial labels become the testimony of a compromise. The ethnic label "Hispanic" is one such compromise. In contrast to African Americans, Hispanics were not an ethnic minority, they became one. The label was imposed, but today it is taken on as the result of a compromise between entrenched racist values and Latino resistance.[13] Still, the Hispanic condition is not a point of departure, but a point of arrival. To this extent, one can say that in inverse relationship to African Americans who are born as such, Hispanics are made, or rather, they become Hispanic. The Hispanic condition is particularly important, not only for personal and existential reasons — given that I am a so-called Hispanic — but also because, as I argue in the following, a series of challenges is presented by it to both American citizenship and to the peoples who are agglutinated under the label "Hispanic."

Many social scientists have rightly pointed to the problems with the ethnic label of "Hispanic."[14] Hispanics are said to be all persons of Latin American descent, who have been in the United States for several generations, or who might have arrived yesterday. They are said to speak Spanish, although many do not. Some are immigrants, while others are political refugees. Some could come from Latin American countries, although it is not clear whether Spaniards and Brazilians could be considered Hispanic. It is also not clear whether Blacks, descendants of slaves from the Caribbean and many Latin American countries with sizable black populations, are either Hispanics or Blacks. In short, the peoples that the label Hispanic hopes to embrace are too heterogeneous and diverse to be done justice to by this rather homogenizing label. Furthermore, as Mary Romero has pointed out, the term Hispanic has contributed to the depoliticization of the history of each group subsumed under the label and it has deleteriously and even disrespectfully placed too much weight on the European elements of the traditions that inform the cultures of peoples of Latin American descent.[15] Indeed, the label "Hispanic" was introduced into the census under President Nixon, precisely at the height of political mobilization and radicalization of Chicanos and Puerto Ricans,[16] and as such it may be interpreted as an attempt to undermine the politicization and radicalization of Latinos.

It is required that we take a closer look at the groups subsumed under the label "Hispanic." Hispanics are made up of peoples of Mexican, Puerto Rican, Cuban, Central and South American, and other Latin American descent. Each group has a very different history, and each one constitutes a different percentage of the more than twenty million Hispanics in the United States. Before proceeding beyond the issue of who gets counted, we must highlight a problem. Should this total number of Hispanics include or exclude Puerto Ricans on the island? If we include the latter, then we accrue another three and a half million so called Hispanics. Nevertheless, if we proceed, we will note that each group constitutes a different percentage of the total number: Mexicans constitute 62.6 percent, Puerto Ricans 11.6 percent, Cubans 7.8 percent, Central and South Americans 12.7 percent and other Hispanics constitute 5.3 percent of the total number of Hispanics.[17] Now, let us consider the three major groups of Hispanics. This will allow us to have a more precise understanding of the problems and challenges that Hispanics have faced and how they pose these problems and challenges to American citizenship.

Mexicans are people that have formed part of the country since the early part of the nineteenth century when the United States colonized the West and Southwest. Through the 1840s, these lands were part of Mexico. After the Mexican-American War, the United States went on to acquire almost half of its present territory by annexing half of Mexico's territory. But Mexicans are also the immigrants that might have just crossed the border. They are a large migrant labor force that cross the border seasonally, in many cases under amnesty. It has been pointed out that sometimes citizenship is extended to new citizens through either immigration or by the result of war. Mexicans became citizens, if only nominally and not in practice, through the effects of imperialistic war.[18] Still, this does not explain the waves of immigration that began to flow with regularity since the turn of the century. With the expansion of the American economy through the first part of this century, and later with the two world wars, the United States actively recruited cheap farm labor in Mexico. This was not just an informal arrangement, but also a national policy. The bracero program, begun in 1943, is a case in point. To this day, despite nativism and xenophobic outbursts against "immigrants," Mexicans continue to be courted by the labor markets of the United States. NAFTA, in fact, must be put in the context of this history of labor assimilation from across the border.

Puerto Ricans have a similar history. They were incorporated into the American body politic in 1898 after the Spanish-American War, when the island of Puerto Rico became a territorial protectorate of the United States. In July of 1898, Guam, Puerto Rico, and the Philippines were turned over by Spain to the United State for a payment of $20 million. Interestingly, however, it was only until the Jones Act of 1917 that American citizenship was effectively imposed upon Puerto Ricans, even though they were deprived of the right to participate in the election of the president that would send them to wars, which was one of the primary reasons for incorporating them as citizens. Nonetheless, like Mexicans, Puerto Ricans have also been actively recruited by the Eastern industrial labor markets. Combined with a policy of industrialization and financial investment that has turned the island into a plantation of U.S economic lords, plus incentives to migrate to the mainland, Puerto Ricans have been left without a homeland, and have yet to be fully accepted in their adoptive country. Puerto Ricans, Mexicans, Native Americans, Hawaiians, and Alaskan Indians, constitute national minorities who have been forcefully brought into the Union only to be made second class citizens. Puerto Ricans, like Native Americans and African Americans, suffer the most severe forms of social privation and stagnation: They have the largest rate of unemployment and the lowest standard of living. Perhaps analogously to Native Americans, most Puerto Ricans are concentrated in their urban reservation: Fort New York.

Cubans, in contrast to Mexicans and Puerto Ricans, came to the United States, partly as a consequence of long-term American policies, but also due to political exile. It is not to be forgotten that Cuba has been under the sphere of American influence since 1898, when the United States challenged the colonial hold of Spain over the Caribbean. Since the Cuban War of Independence, essentially aborted by the Platt Amendment, up through its revolution in 1959, Cuba was an economic colony of the United States. From the revolution, exiles coming from the upper economic classes of Cuban society landed in the United States receiving all kinds of economic aid and sympathy from Americans. At the beginning of the Cold War, Cubans had the "fortune" of being categorized as refugees from a communist regime. Later groups of Cubans coming to the states have not come under such auspicious conditions, yet they have also come as political refugees from a communist dictatorship. Curiously, the imperialism and anticommunism of American history could be said to be summarized and embodied in the history of Cuban immigrants.

Now if we compare these groups, we will note the following similarities and contrasts. While Mexicans have mostly immigrated toward the West and Southwest, Puerto Ricans have concentrated in the tristate area of Connecticut, New York, and Boston, with New York being the primary area of concentration for Puerto Ricans. While a substantive number of Mexicans migrate toward the major metropolises of the West, significant numbers of them gravitate toward the rural labor markets of the West and Southwest. Puerto Ricans, in contrast, remain a mostly urban immigrant population. Cubans, similarly have remained an urban exile community, concentrating in Miami. In contrast to Mexicans, Cubans show the largest and fastest rates of naturalization among Hispanics. Colombians alone show, in absolute numbers, the largest number of naturalizations. Mexicans take the longest to naturalize, when they do. In this they are similar only to Canadians.

Hispanics from Central America and South America have become part of more recent waves of immigrants to the United States in this second half of the twentieth century for reasons similar to those that brought Mexicans, Puerto Ricans, and Cubans to the United States. Thus, if we look at the Nicaraguans, Guatemalans, Salvadoreans, and Costa Ricans, we will notice that they were integrated into the sphere of U.S. influence through either military intervention or economic colonization. The case of Nicaraguans and Guatemalans, however, is a particularly sad chapter in the history of American immigration. Most Nicaraguans and Guatemalans immigrated to the United States aided by relief, peace, and religious organizations. These immigrants were escaping political repression, war, and in many cases violent military persecution and extermination. As is well known today, these conditions were brought about by U.S. policies in Central America, such as direct support of paramilitary organizations in order to destabilize the Sandinista government in Nicaragua. Yet, when most of these political refugees arrived in the United States, they were labeled "illegal aliens" thus not qualifying either for refugee visas or government relief programs such as those that Vietnamese, Cambodians, and now Russians, are receiving.

What should have become patently clear by now is that in all cases, Hispanics have become immigrants due to bidirectional processes having to do with the geopolitics of the United States. In other words, Latin Americans have formed part of the American sphere of influence not only because of foreign policies like the Monroe Doctrine and national self-understanding like the mythology of Manifest Destiny, but also because of more immediate economic and political policies like the bracero and boot strap programs that have actively recruited workers from Mexico and Puerto Rico respectively. In many ways, as Alejandro Portes has aptly put it, many Latin Americans were already Americanized even before they became immigrants.[19] Or, more accurately, they were Hispanicized even before they had become immigrants.

Despite their differences, Hispanics possess the following statistical characteristics. They are younger than the general population. They tend to have lower levels of educational attainment. Over one third of Hispanics tend to be immigrants, which means they tend to be politically isolated. They also have lower levels of employment, and experience the worst working conditions, whether in rural or urban settings. They also tend to earn less than the national average by the large margin of ten thousand dollars. Cubans alone tend to depart from this demographic sketch. From the standpoint of immigration politics and citizenship, Hispanics constitute too heterogeneous a group to make quick generalizations. Some, as we noted, became citizens by being colonized, others by being granted political asylum, and others by immigrating and receiving amnesty. Further, the rates of naturalization varied tremendously between groups. Mexicans are the least likely to naturalize, just as the Colombians are the quickest and most numerous to become citizens. Furthermore, as Portes and Rumbaut note in *Immigrant America*, while turn of the century immigrants came from countries without nationhood, or countries that were in the process of obtaining nationhood, most recent immigrants, especially Latin Americans, arrive in the United States with a strong sense of nationality and of belonging to another national ethos.[20] This has made the process of their acculturation all the more difficult. Most importantly, however, it has hindered the development of a common Hispanic civic culture, or a culture of political participation.

This is the point I want to make: American imperial politics has constituted a veritable underclass that is taking over the role that Blacks occupied in the United States throughout the eighteenth and nineteenth centuries. At the same time, Hispanics have participated in the development, growth, and enrichment of this nation. Hispanics have fought in the wars that this country undertook. Through their labor, enfranchisement, political, and economic struggles, they have also contributed substantively to the transformation and expansion of American democracy. Recognition of this substantive contribution is still forthcoming, even as we approach a new millennium in which Hispanics will constitute more than 15 percent of the U.S. population.

American citizenship, as I hope it has become apparent, faces a serious challenge for Hispanics. Hispanics fit all the categories of a typology of immigrants. They also constitute both "national" and "ethnic" minorities. Some have been citizens since birth, others have yet to become citizens, and some may never do so, although their families might have been American citizens for generations. These different modalities of the Hispanic condition present challenges because as national minorities, Hispanics require particular rights: As ethnic minorities they require special policies to address their entrenched exclusion and marginalization, and as immigrants they also require particular policies that address their unique relationships to the United States. And as citizens-to-be, they call for a policy of civic education and mobilization. American voter participation has been particularly low in the last decades. This apathy will, in effect, become political disenfranchisement if the new Americans are not included, politicized, and conscienticized — to "Anglicize" using Paulo Friere's term — into and through their civic empowerment.

Hispanics, on the other hand, face the challenge of having to disavow obsolete forms of nationalism, to assume a new political consciousness, and even to learn a new form of patriotism, constitutional patriotism, to use Habermas's suggestive expression.[21] Constitutional patriotism not for a nation, was their place of birth, but for the homeland that is their future, and the future of their children. They also face the challenge of having to recognize their unity and commonalities, despite their diverse nationalities and local differences. "Hispanic" is an imposed label. It is certainly not historically conscious or generous. Yet it is one that may allow Latinos to develop a pan-Latin consciousness and a Hispanic American citizenship.

Notes

1. I would like to thank Pedro Lange-Churión, who has been my most important thought partner and critic; Raymond Dennehy, who offered many important suggestions and corrections, and Julio Moreno, who raised questions that I hope to answer in a sequel to this essay.

2. See T. H. Marshall, "Citizenship and Social Class" (1949), reprinted in T. H. Marshall, *Sociology at the Crossroads and Other Essays* (London: Heinemann, 1963).

3. See Jürgen Habermas, "Citizenship and National Identity: Some Reflections on the Future of Europe" in *Praxis International*, 12:1, (April 1992):1–19.

4. See Hagen Schulze, *States, Nations and Nationalism: From the Middle Ages to the Present* (Oxford: Blackwell Publishers Inc., 1996).

5. See T. H. Marshall, "Citizenship and Social Class" and C. B. Macpherson, "Problems of Human Rights in the Late Twentieth Century" in C. B. Macpherson, *The Rise and Fall of Economic Justice and Other Papers* (Oxford: Oxford University Press, 1985).

6. See Michael Walzer, *What it Means to be an American* (New York: Marsilio, 1992), especially the last chapter, "Constitutional Rights and the Shape of Civil Society."

7. See Jürgen Habermas, *Between Facts and Norms: Contributions to a Discourse Theory of Law and Democracy*, trans. William Rehg (Cambridge: MIT Press, 1996).

8. Judith N. Shklar, *American Citizenship: The Quest for Inclusion* (Cambridge: Harvard University Press, 1991).

9. See Rogers M. Smith, *Civic Ideals: Conflicting Visions of Citizenship in U.S. History* (New Haven: Yale University Press, 1997).

10. Linda Martín Alcoff, "Latina/o Identity Politics" in *The Good Citizen* eds. David Batstone and Eduardo Mendieta (New York: Routledge, 1997).

11. J. M. Barbalet, *Citizenship* (Minneapolis: University of Minnesota Press, 1988), 98.

12. See William V. Flores and Rina Benmayor, eds., *Latino Cultural Citizenship* (Boston: Beacon Press, 1997).

13. See Edna Acosta-Belén and Carlos E. Santiago, "Merging Borders: The Remapping of America" in *The Latino Review of Books*, vol. 1, no. 1 (Spring 1995) 2–12.

14. See Suzanne Oboler, *Ethnic Labels, Latino Lives: Identity and the Politics of (Re)Presentation in the United States* (Minneapolis: University of Minnesota Press, 1995); see also Rubín G. Rumbaut, "The Americas: Latin American and Caribbean Peoples in the United States" in *Americas: New Interpretative Essays,* ed. Alfred Stepan (Oxford: Oxford University Press, 1992).

15. Mary Romero, Pierrette Hondagneu-Sotelo, and Vilma Ortiz, eds. *Challenging Fronteras: Structuring Latina and Latino Lives in the U.S.* (New York: Routledge, 1996), xv.

16. See J. Jorge Klor de Alva, "Aztlán, Borinquen and Hispanic Nationalism in the United States" in *Aztlán: Essays on the Chicano Homeland,* eds. Rudolfo A. Anaya and Francisco Lomelí (Albuquerque: University of Mexico Press, 1989).

17. For these statistics see Mary Romero, Pierrette Hondagneu-Sotelo, and Vilma Ortiz, eds., *Challenging Fronteras,* xvii, 106 ff.

18. See Ronald Takaki, *A Different Mirror: A History of Multicultural America* (Boston: Little, Brown and Company, 1993), 166 ff. See also Howard Zinn, *A People's History of the United States* (New York: Harper & Row, 1980), chap. 8.

19. Alejandro Portes, "From South of the Border: Hispanic Minorities in the United States" in *Immigration Reconsidered: History, Sociology, and Politics,* ed. Virginia Yans-McLaughlin, (New York: Oxford University Press, 1990) 162.

20. Alejandro Portes and Rubén G. Rumbaut, *Immigrant America: A Portrait,* 2d ed. (Berkeley: University of California Press, 1996), 107.

21. See Habermas, *Between Facts and Norms,* 465–7, 499–500. I think that Walzer defined just as well this very same concept when he wrote:

> Citizens learn to ask, in addition to their private questions, what the common good really is. In the course of sustained political activity enemies become familiar antagonists, known to be asking the same (contradictory) questions. Men and women who merely tolerated one another's differences recognize that they share a commitment — to *this* arena and to the people in it. Even a divisive election, then, is a

ritual of unity, not only because it has a single outcome, but also because it reaffirms the existence of the arena itself, the public thing, and the sovereign people. Politics is a school of loyalty, through which we make the republic our moral possession and come to regard it with a kind of reverence. And election day is the republic's most important celebration. (Walzer, *What it means to be an American,* p. 100).

NINE

Contagious Word: Paranoia and "Homosexuality" in the Military

★   ★   ★

Judith Butler

The question of whether citizenship requires the repression of homosexuality is not new, but the recent efforts to regulate the self-declaration of homosexuality within the military repose this question in a different light. After all, military personnel enjoy some of the rights and obligations of citizenship, but not all of them. The military is thus already a zone of partial citizenship, a domain in which selected features of citizenship are preserved, and others are suspended. Recent efforts of the U.S. military to impose sanctions on homosexual speech have undergone a series of revisions[1] and at the time of this writing, continue to be contested in court. In the first version of these regulations proposed by the Department of Defense, the term "homosexual" was disallowed as part of a self-ascription or self-definition on the part of military personnel. The term itself was not banished, but only its utterance within the context of self-definition. The very regulation in question, must utter the term in order to perform the circumscription of its usage. The occasion for the formulation of this regulation was, of course, one in which the term "homosexual" already proliferated in military, state, and media discourse. Thus, it is apparently not a problem, within the terms of the regulation, to utter the word: As a consequence of the regulation, in fact, it appears that public discourse on homosexuality has dramatically increased. Indeed, the regulations might be held accountable, paradoxically, for the apparent fact that the word has become more speakable rather than less. And yet the proliferation of public sites in which it has become speakable seems directly tied to the proposal to make it unspeakable in the military as a term that might be taken to describe oneself. The regulations propose the term as unspeakable within the context of self-definition, but they still can only do this by repeatedly proposing the term. Thus, the regulations bring the term into public discourse, rhetorically enunciating the term, performing the circumscription by which — and through which — the term becomes speakable. But the regulations insist as well that there are conditions under which the term is *not* to be insisted on at all, that is, in the service of self-definition. The regulation must conjure one who defines him or herself as a homosexual in order to make plain that no such self-definition is permissible within the military.

The regulation of the term is thus no simple act of censorship or silencing; on the contrary, the regulation redoubles the term it seeks to constrain, and can only effect this constraint through this paradoxical redoubling. The term not only appears in the regulation as that discourse to be regulated, but reappears in the public debate over its fairness and value, specifically as the conjured or imagined act of self-ascription that is explicitly prohibited by the regulation, a prohibition that cannot take place without a conjuring of the very act. We might conclude that the state and the military are merely concerned *to retain control* over what the term will mean, the conditions under which it may be uttered by a speaking subject, restricting that speaking to precisely and exclusively those subjects who are not described by the term they utter. The term is to remain a term used to describe others, but the term is not to be used by those who might use it for the purposes of self-description; to describe oneself by the term is to be prohibited from its use, except in order to deny or qualify the description. The term "homosexual" thus comes to describe a class of persons who are to remain prohibited from defining themselves; the term is to be attributed always from elsewhere. And this is, in some ways, the very

definition of the homosexual that the military and the Congress provide. A homosexual is one whose definition is to be left to others, one
who is denied the act of self-definition with respect to his or her sexuality, one whose self-denial is a prerequisite for military service.

What could account for such a strange regulation of homosexual
locution, one that seems bound to redouble the term at the site of its
prohibition? How do we understand this simultaneous production and
restriction of the term? What is it about the speaking of the term in
the context of self-description that seems more threatening to military
morale than the tacit operation of the sexual practice itself?

The military suspends certain rights for its own personnel that are
accorded to civilians, but that very suspension offers an opportunity
to interrogate what is perhaps most uneasily anchored in, and most
easily jettisoned from, the zone of citizenship. In this sense, one
might consider gays in the military as overlapping with other re-
tractable zones of citizenship: recent immigration law and the suspended zone of citizenship for immigrants, the various degrees of
suspension accorded to different immigrant statuses, not only legal
and illegal, but degrees of legality as well. Such comparisons might
well be considered in relation to Giorgio Agamben's recent thesis that
the state itself has become a protracted "state of emergency," one in
which the claims of citizenship are more or less permanently suspended.[2]

The revisions of the policy on gay speech in the military make clear
how rights based on the First amendment, privacy claims, or the Equal
Protection Clause have been systematically suspended. Whereas Clinton proposed that homosexuals ought only to be excluded from military service to the extent that they engaged in conduct, and not on
the basis of their "status," it became clear in subsequent clarifications
of the policy that stating that one is a homosexual, that is, making reference to one's status is reasonably construed as homosexual conduct
itself. In the Department of Defense Policy, statements are themselves
conduct: according to the more recent Congressional Statute, statements present evidence of a homosexual "propensity" that poses an
unacceptable risk for the military.

It seems clear, as Janet Halley has shown, that arguments that seek to restrict the prosecution of homosexuality to either status or conduct are bound to produce ambiguities that threaten the coherence of either legal basis. In the most recent version of the policy, Halley argues, the question of whether a reasonable person would surmise that another person has a "propensity" to engage in homosexual conduct constitutes the standard by which interrogations proceed. Halley rightly points out that the "reasonable person" is, in this instance, the one who embodies homophobic cultural norms. I would add that this reasonable person is also pervasively paranoid, externalizing a homosexuality that "endangers" the reasonable person from within. It is no longer the case that a statement making reference to one's homosexuality is sufficient to infer the "propensity" to engage in homosexuality: There may be other "signs" — affiliations, gestures, nuances, all of which equally point in the same direction. The "propensity" clause appears to ascribe a natural teleology to homosexual status, whereby we are asked to understand such status as always almost culminating in an act. And yet, this "propensity," though attributed to homosexual status as its natural inclination to express itself, is attributed by the "reasonable" person, and thus remains a figment of the homophobic imaginary.

Although the military now suspects all kinds of signs as indices of "propensity," I will be concentrating on the view of explicit gay self-declaration that the military seeks to prevent, and which it takes to be equivalent to homosexual conduct itself.

The act by which the Department of Defense seeks to circumscribe this act of speech is one that depends on a fabrication of the speech act to be constrained, one in which the fabrication already begins to perform the work of constraint.

In the recent military regulations on homosexual conduct, homosexual self-definition is explicitly construed as contagious and offensive conduct. The words, "I am a homosexual," do not merely describe; they are figured as performing what they describe, not only in the sense that they constitute the speaker as a homosexual, but that they constitute the speech as homosexual conduct. In what follows, I hope to show that the regulation describes as performative the self-ascription of homosexuality, doing precisely that which it says. In describing the power of such acts of utterance, the regulations produce such utterances for us, exercising a performativity that remains the tacit and enabling condition for the delineation of "I am a homosexual" as a performative utterance. Only within that regulatory discourse is the performative power of homosexual self-ascription performatively produced. In this sense, the regulations conjure the spectre of a performative homosexual utterance — an utterance that does the deed — that it seeks to censor, engaging in a circularity of fabrication and censorship that will be specified as paranoid.

If, however, the military can be said to produce a paranoid construal of homosexual utterance as contagious and offensive action, as performing or constituting that to which such utterances refer, how is this attributed performativity to be distinguished from the kind of performativity that is explicitly owned by the movement to authorize greater homosexual publicity, the clear aim of queer politics? According to this latter movement, coming out and acting out are part of the cultural and political meaning of what it is to be homosexual; speaking one's desire, the public display of desire, is essential to the desire itself, the desire cannot be sustained without such speaking and display, and the discursive practice of homosexuality is indissociable from homosexuality itself.

Toward the end of this chapter, I will return to this issue, if only to pose the question of whether homosexuality is not the kind of term that constantly threatens — or promises — to become its own referent, that is, to constitute the very sexuality to which it refers. I hope to suggest that the term cannot fully or exhaustively perform its referent, that no term can, and that "it's a good thing, too." The political benefits to be derived from this incommensurability between performativity and referentiality have to do with setting limits on authoritative constructions of homosexuality and keeping the signifiers of "homosexuality," "gayness," or "queerness," as well as a host of related terms, alive for a future linguistic life. Over and against the commonly stated worry that if homosexuality has no referent, there can be no effective gay and lesbian politics, I would suggest that the absence of a final referent for the term keeps the term from ever being quite as performative as the military imagines that it is. The term gestures toward a referent it cannot capture. Moreover, that lack of capture constitutes the linguistic possibility of a radical democratic contestation, one that opens the term to future rearticulations.[3]

In what sense are the military regulations symptomatic of a paranoia that forms the possibility of military citizenship? The specific performativity attributed to homosexual utterance is not simply that the utterance performs the sexuality of which it speaks, but that it transmits sexuality through speech: The utterance is figured as a site of contagion, a figure that precipitates a return to Freud's *Totem and Taboo* in which the speaking of prohibited names becomes the occasion for an uncontrollable communication. Through recourse to Freud's view of conscience, in which the repression of male homosexuality becomes the prerequisite for constituting manhood, the analysis of the military regulations can be read as producing a notion of the "man" as a self-denying homosexual. Against a psychological reductionism that might locate military acts as acts of individual psyches, I propose to turn to psychoanalysis as a way of reading the text of a highly symptomatic regulation of military citizenship.[4]

Psychoanalysis not only sheds theoretical light on the tensions between homosexuality and citizenship, but psychoanalytic discourse is itself a textual allegory for how the production of the citizen takes place through the rejection and transmutation of an always imagined homosexuality. Indeed, I hope to show that the peculiar form of imagining against oneself which is paranoia constitutes homosexuality not only as a form of inversion, but as the exemplary model for the action of conscience, the turning against oneself that involves the inversion and idealization of the sexual aim. In this sense, Freud's text proves to be as much diagnosis as symptom, and though I propose to read his text psychoanalytically (and, hence, not merely as the enunciation of psychoanalytic practice), I will also be proposing a way to read psychoanalysis allegorically.[5] What this means, more simply, is that Freud will appear to tell us a story about how citizenship and social feeling emerge from the sublimation of homosexuality, but his discourse will be, in the course of this narration, implicated in the very sublimation it describes.[6]

To understand the act of homosexual self-definition as an offense, it seems reasonable to ask, what set of relations or bonds are potentially offended or threatened by such an utterance? It makes sense to turn to Freud's text, "On the Mechanism of Paranoia," in which he links the suppression of homosexual drives to the production of social feeling. At the end of that essay, he remarks that "homosexual drives" help to constitute "the social instincts, thus contributing an erotic factor to friendship and comradeship, to *esprit de corps* and to the love of mankind in general."(31) And at the close of the essay "On Narcissism," he might be read as specifying the logic whereby this production of social feeling takes place. The "ego-ideal," he writes, has a social side:

> It is also the common ideal of a family, a class or a nation. It not only binds the narcissistic libido, but also a considerable amount of the person's homosexual libido, which in this way becomes turned back into the ego. The dissatisfaction due to the non-fulfillment of the ideal liberates homosexual libido, which is transformed into sense of guilt (dread of the community). (81)

This transformation of homosexuality into guilt and, therefore, into the basis of social feeling, takes place when the fear of parental punishment becomes generalized as the dread of losing the love of fellow men. Paranoia is the way in which that love is consistently reimagined as always almost withdrawn, and it is, paradoxically, the fear of losing that love that motivates the sublimation or introversion of homosexuality. Indeed, this sublimation is not quite as instrumental as it may sound, for it is not that one disavows homosexuality in order to gain the love of fellow men, but that it is precisely a certain homosexuality that can be achieved and contained only *through and as* this disavowal.

In Freud's discussion of the formation of conscience in *Civilization and its Discontents,* the very prohibition against homosexuality that conscience is said to enact or articulate is precisely what founds and constitutes conscience itself as a psychic phenomenon. The prohibition against the desire is the desire as it turns back upon itself, and this turning back upon itself becomes the very inception of what is later called "conscience." Hence, what the noun form of "conscience" suggests as a psychic entity, is nothing other than an habituated reflexive activity, the turning back upon oneself, a routing of desire against desire, such that the prohibition becomes the site and satisfaction of desire. That repeated practice of introversion constitutes the misnomer of "conscience" as a mental faculty.

The restrictions on homosexual self-definition suggest that the very circuit of self-prohibition necessary for the production and maintenance of social feeling can no longer be guaranteed by conscience, that conscience is no longer in the service of social regulation. If the military represents a fairly explicit extreme of this regulatory production of homoerotic sociality, it seems that this circuit by which homosexuality is enjoined to turn back on itself again and again has failed to close. This paradox was articulated perhaps most obviously in the claim that social cohesion in the military requires the prohibition on homosexuality, where that cohesion was then described as a magical *je ne sais quoi* that kept military men glued together. The formulation might read: *we must not have our homosexuality in order to have our homosexuality: please take it / don't take it away from us.*

The prohibition that seeks to restrict the outbreak of homosexuality from within this circle of collective introversion figures the very word as a contagious substance, a dangerous fluid. Contagion will be important here, as I will try to show, for homosexuality will be figured implicitly on the model of AIDS, and will be said to "communicate" along the lines of a disease.

The text is overtly one which seeks to regulate homosexual behavior, but as regulatory, it is also incessantly productive. What is conjured in this text is a kind of homosexuality that acts through the magical efficacy of words: to declare that one is a homosexual becomes, within the terms of this law, not merely the representation of conduct, offensive conduct, but offensive conduct itself.

> Sexual orientation will not be a bar to service unless mani-
> fested by homosexual conduct. The military will discharge
> members who engage in homosexual conduct, which is defined
> as a homosexual act, a statement that the member is homosex-
> ual or bisexual, or a marriage or attempted marriage to some-
> one of the same gender.[7]

The statement begins by making a distinction between orientation
and conduct, restricting the military to discharging only those who engage in homosexual conduct. But then homosexual conduct is defined
through a set of appositions which, rather than delimit the barriers of
homosexual conduct, proliferate the possibilities of homosexuality. Homosexual conduct includes "a homosexual act" — even in the singular,
which is to say that it is not yet a practice, a repeated or ritual affair.
And though subsequent clarifications have made clear that a one-time
act, if disavowed as a mistake, will be pardoned, the language of the
policy maintains the one-time requirement, insisting on a conflation of
"act" and "conduct." What is perhaps more properly an *inflation* of act
into conduct is significant, for it tacitly and actively imagines the
singularity of the event as a series of events, a regular practice, and so
imagines a certain force of homosexuality to drive the one-time practi-
tioner into a compulsive or regular repetition. If the act is already conduct, then it has repeated itself before it has any chance to repeat; it
is, as it were, always already repeating, a figure for a repetition —
compulsion with the force to undermine all sorts of social morale.

Let us return to the phrasing in order to read this passage as an articulation of a homophobic phantasmatic:

> The military will discharge members who engage in homosex-
> ual conduct, which is defined as a homosexual act, a statement
> that the member is homosexual or bisexual, or a marriage or at-
> tempted marriage to someone of the same gender.

Homosexual conduct, defined as "a statement that the member is
homosexual or bisexual"; in this definition the "statement" is a form of
"conduct," and new meaning is given to MacKinnon's reference to

"only words." If the statement is conduct, and it is homosexual conduct, then the statement that one is a homosexual is construed as acting homosexually on the person to whom or before whom it is
uttered. The statement is in some sense not only an act, but a form of
conduct, a ritualistic form of speech that wields the power to *be* what
it *says*, not a re-presentation of a homosexuality, but a homosexual act
and, hence, an offense. Under what conditions does an utterance that
represents a disposition or a practice become that very disposition
and practice, a becoming, a transitivity, that depends on and institutes
the collapse of the distinction between speech and conduct? This is
not to say that an absolute distinction between speech and conduct
might be drawn. On the contrary, that a statement is a kind of act, a
speech act, is true enough, but that is not the same as claiming that
the statement perforce enacts what it says or constitutes the referent
to which it refers. Many speech acts are "conduct" in a narrow sense,
but not all of them are felicitous in the sense that Austin maintains.
That is, not all of these acts have the power to produce effects or initiate a set of consequences.

The utterance which claims or proclaims homosexual identity is
construed as offensive conduct only if we concede that something
about the very speaking of homosexuality in the context of self-definition is disruptive. But what gives such words the disruptive power
they are presumed to wield? Does such a presumption not imply that
the one who hears the utterance imagines him/herself to be solicited
by the statement? In a sense, the reception traces the Foucaultian formulation in reverse: If Foucault thought that there were first homosexual "acts" and only later did homosexuality emerge as an "identity,"
then the military takes every ascription of identity as equivalent to the
doing of an act. It is important to distinguish, however, between two
ways of rethinking identity as act: where one might say that what I
mean by saying that "I am a homosexual" is that "I perform homosexual acts, or engage in homosexual practices or relationships," I would
still be referring to those acts, but not, strictly speaking, performing
them and certainly not performing them through the act of speaking.
The military reading of the claim, however, appears to be of another
order. That reading takes the claim, "I am a homosexual" to be one of

the very acts of homosexuality, not a reporting on the happening of acts, but the discursive happening of the act itself.

In what sense is the act "conduct"? Surely, one might claim that any locution is "conduct," and Austin concedes that all utterance is in some sense an "act." But even if every utterance can be construed as an act, it does not follow that all utterance *acts upon* its listener in a prescribed or mechanical way; the problem of "uptake" in Austin underscores the contingent dimension of all such appropriation regarding perlocutionary performatives. But are there situations in which the contingency, the interpretive diversity, and potential failure of "uptake" appears to be determined by the force of the utterance? And is the proclamation, "I am a homosexual," an instance of such a determining utterance?

The problem of uptake is displaced from view when the performative force attributed to the utterance becomes overdetermined in fantasy. Such an overdetermination takes place in the paranoid fantasy by which the military construes homosexual utterance to take place. The statement, then, "I am a homosexual," is fabulously misconstrued as, "I want you sexually." A claim that is, in the first instance, reflexive, that attributes a status only to oneself, is taken to be solicitous, that is, a claim that announces availability or desire, the intention to act, the act itself: the verbal vehicle of seduction. In effect, a desirous intention is attributed to the statement or the statement is itself invested with the *contagious* power of the magical word, whereby to hear the utterance is to "contract" the sexuality to which it refers. The presumption here is that when and if the term, "homosexual," is claimed for oneself, it is in the service not only of a statement of desire, but becomes the discursive condition and vehicle of the desire, transferring that desire, arousing that desire. This is a statement construed as a solicitation; a constative taken as an interrogative; a self-ascription taken as an address.

Presumed in the military construal of the self-defining statement as offensive action is that the speakability of the term breaks a taboo within public discourse, the floodgates open, and expressions of desire become uncontrollable. Hence, the one before whom the desire under taboo is spoken becomes immediately afflicted by the desire

borne by the word; to speak the word before such a person is to impli-
cate that person in unspeakable desire. The word — and the desire —
is caught in precisely the way in which a disease is said to be caught.
Within contemporary military discourse, the taboo status of homosexuality is intensified by the phobic reduction of homosexual relations
to the communication of AIDS, intensifying the sense of homosexual
proclamations as contagious acts.

Indeed, consider the salience of the metaphor of contagion for
Freud's discussion of taboo in *Totem and Taboo*:

> Taboo is a . . . prohibition imposed (by some authority) from
> outside, and directed against the most powerful longings to
> which human beings are subject. The desire to violate it per-
> sists in their unconscious; those who obey the taboo have an
> ambivalent attitude to what the taboo prohibits. The magical
> power that is attributed to taboo is based on the capacity for
> arousing temptation; and it acts like a contagion because exam-
> ples are contagious and because the prohibited desire in the
> unconscious shifts from one thing to another. (35)

In this last remark, Freud makes clear that the prohibited desire in
the unconscious shifts from one thing to another, is itself an uncon-
trollably transferable desire, subject to a metonymic logic that is not
yet constrained by the law. Indeed, it is the incessant transferability of
this desire that is instituted by the taboo, and that informs the logic of
contagion by which the desire under taboo enters into discourse as a
highly communicable name. If I say, "I am a homosexual," in front of
you, then you become implicated in the "homosexuality" that I utter;
the utterance is presumed to establish a relationship between the
speaker and the audience, and if the speaker is proclaiming homosexuality, then that discursive relationship becomes constituted by virtue
of that utterance, and that very homosexuality is communicated in the
transitive sense. The utterance appears both to communicate and
transfer that homosexuality (becomes itself the vehicle for a displacement onto the addressee) according to a metonymic rush which is, by
definition, beyond conscious control. Indeed, the sign of its *uncon-*

scious status is precisely that it "communicates" or "transfers" between speaker and audience in precisely that uncontrollable way.

Earlier in this same text, Freud refers to "dangerous attributes" applied indifferently and simultaneously to persons, their states, their acts; the attribute not only shifts between these registers, but it becomes tempting and terrifying precisely by virtue of this shiftiness: "Anyone who has violated a taboo becomes taboo himself because he possesses the dangerous quality of tempting others to follow his example: why should he be allowed to do what is forbidden to others? Thus he is truly contagious in that every example encourages imitation . . . ."(32) Freud distinguishes between those kinds of taboos invested with contagious power that "produce temptation and encourage imitation" and another in which the transmissability of a taboo is its displacement onto material objects. (34) These two forms converge later, however, when he refers to taboo names as that material instance of language that carries both the desire and its prohibition, that is, that becomes the discursive site for the displacement of ambivalence. The "transmissability of taboo" is a function of metonymic displacement, "the tendency . . . for the unconscious instinct . . . to shift constantly along associative paths on to new objects."(34)

The question that emerges in trying to read the logic of contagion as it operates within the military ban on homosexual statements and acts is how a name and the act of self-naming in particular becomes precisely such a material/discursive carrier for this displacement and "transmissability." The sign uttered in the service of a prohibition carries that prohibition and becomes speakable only in the service of that prohibition. The breaking of the prohibition through the uttering of the sign becomes, then, a disjoining of that sign from its prohibitive function, and an unconscious transfer of the desire that the sign has, until this resignification, kept in check. The name, "homosexual," is not merely a sign of desire, but becomes the means by which desire is absorbed into and carried by the sign itself. The sign, in the service of prohibition, has substituted for the desire it represents, but also has acquired a "carrier" function that links homosexuality with contagion. It is, of course, not difficult to imagine which one. How are we to account for this symbolic conflation of the fluidity of the sign and "dangerous fluids"? Homosexuality, within this paranoid metonymy, has become a paradigm for contagion. The self-descriptive utterance of "homosexuality" becomes the very act of dangerous communication which, participating in a contemporary revaluation of that sacred scene, infects its listener — immaculately — through the ear.

Freud concludes his remarks with the reminder that the taboo can be reinstalled only through the speech act that *renounces* desire: "The fact that the violation of a taboo can be atoned for by a renunciation shows that renunciation lies at the basis of obedience to taboo."(35) In a corollary move, the military makes provisions for those who would recant their indiscretion; the only way to counter the public force and threat of a public act of self-definition as a homosexual is through an equally public self-renunciation. In remarks intended to clarify how the policy would be implemented, the military makes clear that to assert one is a homosexual presents a "rebuttable presumption" that one will act in a homosexual way. In other words, one may now say, "I am a homosexual and I intend not to act on my desire," and in such a case, the first clause, "I am a homosexual," loses its performative force; its constative status is restored through the addition of the second clause. In Freud, the renunciation takes the form of regret and atonement, but it makes no claims to having annihilated the desire; indeed, within renunciation, the desire is kept intact, and there is a strange and important way in which prohibition might be said to *preserve* desire.

In *Civilization and its Discontents*, the repression of the libido is itself a libidinally-invested repression. The libido is not absolutely negated through repression, but rather becomes the instrument of its own subjection. The repressive law is not external to the libido that it represses, but the repressive law represses to the extent that repression becomes a libidinal activity.[8] Further, moral interdictions, especially those that are turned against the body, are themselves sustained by the very bodily activity that they seek to curb:

> An idea . . . which belongs entirely to psychoanalysis and which is foreign to people's ordinary way of thinking . . . it tells

us that conscience (or more correctly, the anxiety which later becomes conscience) is indeed the cause of instinctual renunciation to begin with, but that later that relationship is reversed. Every renunciation of instinct now becomes a dynamic source of conscience and every fresh renunciation increases the latter's severity and intolerance. (CD, 84)

According to Freud the self-imposed imperatives that characterize the circular route of conscience are pursued and applied precisely because they become the site of the very satisfaction they seek to prohibit. In other words, prohibition becomes the displaced site of satisfaction for the "instinct" or desire that is prohibited, an occasion for the reliving of the instinct under the rubric of the condemning law. This is of course the source of that form of comedy in which the bearer of the moral law turns out to be the most serious transgressor of its precepts. And precisely because this displaced satisfaction is experienced through the application of the law, that application is reinvigorated and intensified with the emergence of every prohibited desire. The prohibition does not seek the obliteration of prohibited desire; on the contrary, prohibition pursues the reproduction of prohibited desire and becomes itself intensified through the renunciations it effects. The afterlife of prohibited desire takes place through the prohibition itself, where the prohibition not only sustains, but is *sustained by*, the desire that it forces into renunciation. In this sense, then, renunciation takes place *through* the very desire that is renounced, which is to say that the desire is never renounced, but becomes preserved and reasserted in the very structure of renunciation. The renunciation by which the military citizen is purged of his sin and reestablished in his or her place, then, becomes the act by which the prohibition at once denies and concedes homosexual desire; it is not, strictly speaking, *un*speakable, but is, more generally, retained in the speaking of the prohibition. In the case of the homosexual who claims to be one, but insists that he or she will not act on his or her desire, the homosexuality persists in and as the application of that prohibition to oneself. This is, interestingly, how Paul Ricueur once described the psychic circuit of hell: a vicious circle of desire and interdiction.

And it may be that the military "regulation" is an intensified cultural site for the continuing theological force of that interdiction.

But consider how it is that a term or the proclamation of an identity might be understood discursively to carry or cause an injury. What is the theory of causation in this instance, and is this a "cause" established in paranoia? Freud offers the following account of how it is that paranoia is *caused*, but not in the analysis of how the causal account of paranoia slides into the paranoid account of causation. He writes, "paranoia is a disorder in which a sexual aetiology is by no means obvious; on the contrary, the strikingly prominent features in the causation of paranoia, especially among males, are social humiliations and slights. . . . " So far Freud appears to be substituting a true for a false cause of paranoia: It appears that what causes paranoia are slights and injuries, but what truly causes paranoia is a sexual wish subject to an introversion; the imagined punishment by others is the idealized and exteriorized effect of a prohibition against one's desire that is at the origin of that idealization and exteriorization. The agency of that prohibition is in some sense displaced, and the reasons for the beratement have already become illegible. Freud then continues, claiming that if we go into the matter "more deeply," we shall see that "the really operative factor in these social injuries lies in the part played in them by the homosexual components of affective life."(30)

It is this last phrase that introduces ambiguity into Freud's account. For how are we to understand how "homosexual components of affective life play a part in these social injuries"? To feel slighted or injured, to imagine oneself slighted or injured, how precisely is this to be read as a permutation of homosexuality? Is the slight, the injury, the imagined external form that the prohibition against homosexuality takes, and is one being slighted and injured by virtue of one's homosexual desires? Or is this being slighted and injured an imagining of the social injury to which an exposed homosexual might very well be subject? The uncertainty appears to be this: Is the prohibition a social one that might be said to become diffuse and generalized, or is it a psychic and internal one that becomes externalized and generalized in the course of paranoia?

In the first instance, it is the social vulnerability of the homosexual to injury that is projected onto a more generalized sense of others as berating and slighting in their behavior; but in the latter case, it is the psychic sublimation of homosexuality that creates the very notion of the social, the notion of Others as regulating, watching, and judging, an imaginary scenario which becomes what is known as "conscience" and prepares the subject for that social feeling that supports citizenship. The two possible sequences differ dramatically in their consequences. The second view postulates a homosexual desire that turns against itself, and then produces a notion of the social as a consequence of that turning back against itself: Social feeling, understood here as coextensive with social regulation, is a consequence of sublimated homosexuality, the projection and generalization of a set of judging and watching Others. This is a formulation that postulates homosexuality as the outside to the social, as the presocial, and derives the social, understood as a primarily regulatory domain, from the self-suppression of this sexuality.

But how are we to understand this self-suppression apart from the social regulations by which homosexuality is itself cast as the asocial, the presocial, the impossibility of the social within the social? If the two versions of prohibition (psychic and social) cannot be dissociated from one another, how are they to be thought together? The slights and injuries experienced within what is called paranoia are the psychic traces of existing social regulations, even as those traces have become estranged from the regulations from which they are derived. The slights and injuries are not only the effects of a desire turned back on itself, and the subsequent projection of those turned back desires onto the judgments of others (Indeed a blending of super-egoic functions with social ones); rather, it is the coincidence of the judgment of Others and that turning back upon oneself that produces the imaginary scenario in which the condemned and unlived desire registers psychically as the imagined slights and injuries performed by Others.

Thus, the turn to Freud is not an effort to read Freud as the truth of homosexuality, but, rather, as a way to exemplify or allegorize the circularity in the account of paranoia, a circularity that comes to afflict Freud's own account. For instance, in "On the Mechanism of Paranoia," he writes approvingly of the way in which homosexual feelings are necessary to the love of mankind, how they euphemistically "combine" with the instincts for self-preservation to produce "man" in the "proper sense" of that term. If, to use his terms, homosexual tendencies "combine with" ego-instincts, where ego-instincts are defined as self-preservative, then it becomes part of the project of "man's" self-preservation — the preservation of "man, properly speaking" — to deflect, and preserve in deflection, his homosexuality. (69) Hence, the etiology that Freud offers us is already within the normative and regulatory domain of the social for which he seeks to give an account. It is not that there are first homosexual feelings which then combine with self-preservative instincts, but that, according to the social norms that govern the conditions of self-preservation *as a man*, homosexuality must remain a permanently deflected possibility. Hence, it is not man's homosexuality that helps to constitute his social instincts, and his general mindfulness of others, but, rather, the repression or deflection of the ostensible narcissism of homosexuality that is construed as the condition for altruism, understood as one of the benefits of an accomplished heterosexuality. In this sense, the desexualization and externalization of homosexuality makes for a "man" — properly speaking — who will always feel slights and injuries in the place where homosexual desire might have lived, and for whom this transposition of desire into imagined injury will become the basis of social feeling and citizenship. Note that this unacted homosexuality becomes the condition for sociality and the love of mankind in general.

It is not simply that homosexuality must remain unacted and deflected such that man in his self-preserving and proper sense may live, but that the very notion of the "ego-ideal" — the imaginary measure by which citizenship is psychically regulated — is itself composed of this unacted and deflected homosexuality. The ego-ideal is formed through the withdrawal of large quantities of homosexual cathexis.[9] This homosexuality, however, is neither simply withdrawn nor simply deflected or repressed, but, rather turned back on itself, and this turning back on itself is not a simple self-cancellation; on the contrary, it is the condition for the fabrication of the ego-ideal in which homosexuality and its prohibition "combine" in the figure of the heterosexual citizen, one whose guilt will be more or less permanent. Indeed Freud will say that homosexual libido is "transformed into sense of guilt" and citizenship itself — the attachment to and embodiment of the law — will be derived from this guilt.

How, then, do we return to the problem that emerges within the military, where the military is at once a zone of suspended citizenship, and one which, by virtue of this suspended status, articulates in graphic terms the production of the masculinist citizen through the prohibition on homosexuality. Although the military regulations appear to figure homosexuality in masculinist terms, it is clear that lesbians are targeted as well, but that, paradoxically, the interrogations into their personal life often take the form of sexual harassment. In other words, women cannot speak their homosexuality because that would be to threaten the heterosexual axis along which gender subordination is secured. And if men speak their homosexuality, that speaking threatens to bring into explicitness and, hence, destroy, the homosociality by which the class of men coheres.

The line that demarcates the speakable from the unspeakable instates the current boundaries of the social. Could the uttering of the word constitute a slight, an injury, indeed, an offense, if the word did not carry the sedimented history of its own suppression? In this sense, the word becomes an "act" precisely to the extent that its unspeakability circumscribes the social. The speaking of the word outside its prohibition calls into question the integrity and the ground of the social as such. In this way, the word contests the boundaries of the social, the repressive ground of the citizen subject by naming the relation that must be assumed for that sociality to emerge, but which can only produce that sociality by remaining unnamed. Unwittingly, it seems, the military introduces that word into its contagious circuit precisely through the prohibition which is supposed to secure its unspeakability. And it is in this way that the military speaks its desire again and again at the very moment, through the very terms, by which it seeks its suppression.

In fact, it is crucial to consider that the military does not merely confront the homosexual as a problem to be regulated and contained, but it actively produces this figure of the homosexual, insisting that this homosexual be deprived of the power of self-ascription, remaining named and animated by the state and its powers of interpellation. In its military dimension, the state insists on the codification of homosexuality. The homosexual subject is brought into being through a discourse that at once names that "homosexuality" and produces and defines this identity as an infraction against the social. But where it names this subject compulsively, it denies to this subject the power to name itself; thus the state seeks to curb not merely homosexual actions, but the excessive power of the name when it becomes unshackled from the prohibitions by which it is spawned. What and who will the name describe on the occasion when it no longer serves the disciplinary aims of military nomination?

How, then, do we think about the situation in which the self-ascription, the reflexive statement, "I am a homosexual," is misconstrued as a seduction or an assault, one in which a desire is not merely described but, in being described, is understood to be enacted and conveyed? In the first instance, I think we must read this construal of homosexuality and homosexual acts as assault and/or disease as an effort to circumscribe homosexuality within that pathologizing set of figurations. This is not simply an account of how the words of homosexuals performatively produce homosexuality, but, as state-sanctioned figure, a restrictive definition of homosexuality as an assaultive and contagious action. Hence, the performativity attributed to the homosexual utterance can only be established through the performativity of a state discourse that makes this very attribution. The figuring of homosexual utterance as contagion is a performative sort of figuring, a performativity that belongs to regulatory discourse. Does the statement reveal the performative power of homosexual utterance, or does it merely underscore the productive or performative power of those who exercise the power to define homosexuality in these terms?

This discursive power to enforce a definition of the homosexual is one that finally belongs neither to the military nor to those who oppose it. After all, I have just produced the military production for you and entered into the chain of performativity that I've been charting, implicating myself in the reproduction of the term, with far less power, admittedly, than those whose acts I describe. Is anything like homosexuality being described in this chain of performativity? Perhaps it is a mistake to claim that we might have the power to produce an authoritative or affirmative notion of homosexuality when we go about naming it, naming ourselves, defining its terms. The problem is not merely that homophobic witnesses to self-proclaiming homosexuals hallucinate the speaking of the word as the doing of the deed, but that even those who oppose the military are willing to accept the notion that naming is performative, that to some extent it brings into linguistic being that which it names. There does seem to be a sense in which speech acts and speech, more generally, might be said to constitute conduct, and that the discourse produced about homosexuality is part of the social constitution of homosexuality as we know it. Conventional distinctions between speech and conduct do collapse when, for instance, what we might loosely call representation *is* coextensive with, say, being "out" as a cultural practice of gayness and queerness, between cultural representations that express homosexuality and homosexuality "itself." It would, after all, be somewhat reductive to claim that homosexuality is only sexual behavior in some very restricted sense, and that there is then, superadded to this behavior, a set of representations of homosexuality that, strictly speaking, *are not* homosexuality proper. Or are they?

Many would want to argue that homosexuality and its cultural representation are *not* dissociable, that representation does not follow sexuality as its dim reflection, but that representation has a constitutive function, and that, if anything, sexuality follows representation as one of its effects: This appears to be the presumption in the claim that public conventions organize and make possible "sexuality" and that the acts, and the cultural practices that orchestrate and sustain the acts, as it were, cannot be strictly distinguished. To construe sexuality as an "act" is already to abstract from a cultural practice, a reiterative ritual, in which it takes place and of which it is an instance. Indeed, the very notion of a sexual practice is precisely that which overrides the distinction between "act" and "representation."

To insist, however, that discourse on homosexuality, including the discursive act of "coming out," is part of what is understood, culturally, as "homosexuality" is not quite the same as claiming that saying one is homosexual is itself a homosexual act, much less a homosexual offense. Although I think we can imagine queer activists who would claim that the self-appellation is a sexual act in some broadly inter-preted sense of that term, there is a certain comedy that emerges when "queer" becomes so utterly disjoined from sexual practice that every well-meaning heterosexual takes on the term. But we surely need to take seriously the contention that "coming out" is intended as a contagious example, that it is supposed to set a precedent and incite a series of similarly structured acts in public discourse. The military may be responding precisely to the felicitous perlocutionary conse-quences of coming out, the way in which the example has spawned a rash of coming outs throughout the public sphere, proliferating itself as if it were a certain kind of linguistic contagion — a contagion, we might conjecture, that is meant in part to counter the force of that other contagion, namely, AIDS. What, then, is the difference between the logic that governs the military policy and the one which governs queer activism?

One way of understanding this, I think, is to note the way in which paranoid military listening consistently closes the gap between the speaking of a desire and the desire that is being spoken. The one ap-pears to communicate the other directly in moments of seduction (but even there we know through painful examples that the communica-tion is not always interpreted in quite the right way); in paranoia, though, the desire that the speaking elicits is imagined as emerging wholly and without solicitation from the one who speaks it. It comes from the outside, as an assault, or as a disease, and becomes regis-tered as injury and/or contamination. Hence, the desire is already fig-ured as assault or disease, and can be received in one form or the other, or both. How is that figuration to be understood as different from the production of a discourse about homosexuality, which might work against this pathological reduction and constitute a socially affir-mative meaning for homosexuality?

Here is where I want to argue for the notion that a discursive pro-duction of homosexuality, a talking about, a writing about, and institu-tional recognition of, homosexuality, is not exactly the same as the desire of which it speaks. Whereas the discursive apparatus of homosexuality constitutes its social reality, it does not constitute it fully. The declaration that is "coming out" is certainly a kind of act, but it does not fully constitute the referent to which it refers; indeed, *it renders homosexuality discursive, but it does not render discourse referential.* This is not to say that desire is a referent that we might describe in some other or better way; on the contrary, it is a referent that sets a certain limit to referential description in general, one that nevertheless compels the chain of performativity by which it is never quite captured. In an effort to preserve this sense of desire as a limit to referentiality, it is important not to close the gap between the performative and the referential and to think that by proclaiming homosexuality, homosexuality itself becomes nothing other than the proclamation by which it is asserted. Although Foucault might claim that discourse becomes sexualized through such an act, it may be that discourse is precisely what desexualizes homosexuality in this instance.[10] My sense is that this kind of account of the discursive production of homosexuality makes the mistake of substituting the name for what it names, and though that referent cannot be finally named, it must be kept separate from what is nameable, if only to guarantee that no name claims finally to exhaust the meaning of what we are and what we do, an event that would foreclose the possibility of becoming more and different than what we have already become, in short, foreclose the future of our life within language, a future in which the signifier remains a site of contest, available to democratic rearticulation.

In this sense, I would argue that the discourse about homosexual desire is not, strictly speaking, the same as the desire that it speaks, and when we think that we are acting homosexually when we speak about homosexuality we are, I think, making a bit of a mistake. For one of the tasks of a critical production of alternative homosexualities will be to disjoin homosexuality from the figures by which it is conveyed in dominant discourse, especially when they take the form of either assault or disease. Indeed, as much as it is necessary to produce other figures, to continue the future of performativity and, hence, of homosexuality, it will be the distance between something called "homosexuality" and that which cannot be fully interpellated through such a call that will undermine the power of any figure to be the last word on homosexuality. And it is that last word, I think, that is most important to forestall.

Notes

This essay, while originally intended for inclusion in this collection, is also reprinted from *Excitable Speech: A Politics of the Performative,* pp. 103–126, Routledge: 1997, by kind permission of the author.

1. The Pentagon announced its "New Policy Guidelines on Homosexuals in the Military" on 19 July 1993, which included the following "discharge" policy: "Sexual orientation will not be a bar to service unless manifested by homosexual conduct. The military will discharge members who engage in homosexual conduct, which is defined as a homosexual act, a statement that the member is homosexual or bisexual, or a marriage or attempted marriage to someone of the same gender." After discussions in Congress on the policy, the Department of Defense on 22 December 1993 issued a set of new regulations seeking to clarify problems concerning implementation of the policy. One of the key issues to be clarified was whether a "statement" to the effect that one is a homosexual can be taken not only as "conduct" but as sufficient grounds for dismissal from the military. The clarification offered by the Department of Defense made clear that "statements that can be a basis for discharge are those which demonstrate a propensity or intent to engage in acts." Over and against those who claim that statements of the desire or intentions of an individual are not the same as conduct, the Department of Defense insisted that what they now have is "a conduct-based policy," on that is based on "the likelihood that the person would act." They explain, "a statement creates a rebuttable presumption a person will engage in acts, but the service member then has an opportunity to rebut. . . ."

Here, the "statement" that one is a homosexual presents the occasion to rebut the presumption, but later in this same presentation, the spokesperson from the Department of Defense appears to suggest the opposite: "Associational activities, like going to a gay parade or reading a magazine — in and of themselves — are not credible information [bearing on the conduct of the individual in question], and only rise to that level if they are such that a reasonable person would believe that *the conduct was intended to make a statement, intended to tell other people that the person is a homosexual*" (my emphasis). Here the question appears no longer to be whether the statement presents a rebuttable presumption that the person will engage in conduct, but whether conduct, of an associational kind, is sufficient to establish that a statement is being made. Whether the basis for dismissal is statement or conduct remains effectively open (20 July 1993; 22 Dec. 1993, *New York Times*).

In addition to the former and current Department of Defense policy, Congress entered the fray by introducing legislation of its own: The National Defense Authorization Act for Fiscal Year 1994. This binding statute emphasizes the problem of homosexual "propensity," and states that persons who demonstrate a propensity to act homosexually are deemed incompatible with military service. The statute also shows leniency for those who commit such acts on an occasion, but who repent or claim it was an accident. It also reintroduces the obligation of military officers "to ask" servicemen about their orientation. Whereas it does not accept statements regarding one's own homosexuality as tantamount to homosexual acts, it does regard such statements as *evidence of a propensity* that poses a rebuttable presumption of homosexuality.

Recent rulings on the new policy have split on the question of whether First Amendment rights are denied by the policy (suits concerning the "old policy" continue to be litigated as well, with mixed results). For a thorough and incisive review of this litigation, one on which I heavily rely in this discussion, see Janet Halley, "The Status/Conduct Distinction in the 1993 Revisions to Military Anti-Gay Policy" in *GLQ,* Winter, 1996.

2. Giorgio Agamben, "States of Emergency," lecture at the University of California at Berkeley, November, 1995.

3. Ernesto Laclau and Chantal Mouffe, *Hegemony and Socialist Strategy*, (London: Verso, 1986).

4. The following texts by Sigmund Freud are cited in this chapter: "On the Mechanism of Paranoia," (1911) and "On Narcissism: An Introduction" (1914), from *General Psychological Theory: Papers on Metapsychology* (New York: MacMillan, 1963) 29–48 and 56–82, respectively; *Civilization and its Discontents*, tr. James Strachey, (New York: Norton, 1961); and *Totem and Taboo*, tr. James Strachey, (New York: Norton, 1950).

5. By allegory, I mean a kind of narrative in which, most generally, one speaks otherwise than one appears to speak, where one offers a sequential

narrative ordering for something that cannot be described sequentially, and where the apparent referent of the allegory becomes the very action of elaboration that allegorical narrative performs.

6. For an interesting and relevant account of allegory, see Craig Owens, *Beyond Recognition: Representation, Power, and Culture*, ed. Scott Bryson (Berkeley: University of California Press, 1992).

7. "The Pentagon's New Policy Guidelines on Homosexuals in the Military," *New York Times*, 20 July 1993, A14.

8. Here one can see that Foucault's critique of Freud in *The History of Sexuality, Volume I* is partially wrong.

9. Sigmund Freud, "On Narcissism: An Introduction," *Standard Edition* vol. XIV (London: Hogarth Press, 1957), 96.

10. This would be a way to both confirm and deny the recent suggestions by Leo Bersani in *Homos* (Cambridge: Harvard University Press, 1995) that asserting a stable identity is a precondition of gay activism and that the intellectual skepticism directed at the success of that speech act are complicitous with a desexualization of gayness. To come out is still to perform a linguistic act and, hence, not necessarily to have sex or be sexual, except in that discursive way that may constitute a further instance of the linguistic sublimation of sex that Bersani laments.

Acknowledgments

★ ★ ★

This book would not have been possible without the support of the University of San Francisco, and its Louise M. Davies Forum on *The Search for Values in Contemporary America*. The University of California Berkeley Extension Program also was instrumental in sponsoring and promoting the lecture series that provided the inspiration for this book. Out of these two institutions we especially acknowledge the contributions of the following people: Stanley Nel, Gerardo Marín, Michael Webber, Alice Boatwright, and Bula Maddison. We acknowledge as well our Davies Scholars, who contributed to this book by joining in our seminar in the classroom and on-line.

We also want to thank each contributor to this volume. In all cases, they took time from their busy schedules to reflect on the changing meanings of citizenship. David thanks James Daly and Jeffrey Davis at *Business 2.0* for their insight and inspiration. Eduardo thanks Pedro Lange-Churión, Julio Moreno, and Ray Dennehy, Martin Woessner, and Anna Maria Belda for their inspiration, challenging criticisms, ecumenism, and skills with computers, words, and photocopiers. Finally, we especially recognize Bill Germano at Routledge, who from the start believed in this project, and who has been supportive, understanding, and humorous.

David Batstone

Eduardo Mendieta

The University of San Francisco
San Francisco, California

Contributors

★   ★   ★

Linda Martín Alcoff   Associate Professor of Philosophy at Syracuse University. She has coedited *Feminist Epistemologies* (Routledge, 1993) and written *Real Knowing: New Versions of the Coherence Theory of Knowledge* (1996), and edited *Epistemology: The Big Questions* (1998). She has written over twenty articles on topics concerning Foucault, sexual violence, the politics of knowledge, gender and race identity, and is at work on a new book entitled *Visible Identities*. She received an ACLS Fellowship for 1990–1991 and a fellowship from the Society for the Humanities at Cornell University for 1994–1995. In 1995 she was awarded a Laura J. and Douglas Meredith Professorship to recognize outstanding teaching at Syracuse University.

David Batstone   Associate Professor of Social Ethics at the University of San Francisco, Batstone is author of *From Conquest to Struggle* (1992), editor of *New Visions for the Americas* (1994), and coeditor of *Liberation Theologies, Postmodernity and the Americas* (Routledge, 1997).

Batstone is Editor-at-Large for *Business 2.0* magazine, and has written for the *Sunday Chicago Tribune*, *SPIN*, the *New York Times* and *Wired*. His radio series, "What Does it Mean to Be an American?" airs on National Public Radio stations across the country.

In 1996, Batstone was named the National Endowment for the Humanities Chair at the University of San Francisco for his work in technology and ethics, and the following year established the Global Cafe, a nationally acclaimed on-line learning site.

Robert N. Bellah   *Newsweek* magazine called his *Habits of the Heart* (1986) a "brilliant analysis" and "the most readable study of American society since David Riesman's '50s classic *The Lonely Crowd*."

Professor of Sociology Emeritus at the University of California, Berkeley, Bellah has practically framed the terms of the American debate regarding individualism and social obligation with his books *The Good Society* (1991), *Beyond Belief* (1970), *The Broken Covenant* (1992), *Varieties of Civil Religion* (1980), and *On Morality and Society* (1973).

Judith Butler Butler writes on questions of identity politics, gender and sexuality, most notably in her books *Subjects of Desire* (1987), *Gender Trouble* (Routledge, 1990), *Feminists Theorize the Political* (Routledge, 1992), and *Bodies That Matter* (Routledge, 1993). She has had a major impact on political activists in the United States and Europe. Having received her doctorate from Yale University, Butler taught at The John Hopkins University and is currently a Professor of Rhetoric at the University of California, Berkeley.

Barbara Christian Professor of Afro-American Studies at the University of California, Berkeley. The *Sunday Chicago Tribune* named her "one of this country's most important critics of black culture and literature."

Christian has authored *A Teaching Guide to accompany Black Foremothers* (1980), *Black Women Novelists* (1980), *Black Feminist Criticism* (1985), *Alice Walker's The Color Purple and Other Works* (1987), and is writing a major book on the life and work of Toni Morrison. Christian is an editor of the *Norton Anthology of Black Literature*.

Michael Lerner Lerner is founder and editor of *Tikkun*, critically acclaimed for its treatment of politics and social values. A frequent lecturer in universities and religious communities across the country, he is the author of *Surplus Powerlessness* (1991), *The Socialism of Fools: Anti-Semitism on the Left* (1992), *Jewish Renewal: A Path to Healing and Transformation* (1994), *The Politics of Meaning* (1996), and, along with Cornel West, *Jews and Blacks: Let the Healing Begin* (1995).

Lerner is also the founder of the Institute for Labor and Mental Health.

Eduardo Mendieta Mendieta was born in Colombia and emigrated with his parents to the United States in the late seventies. Assistant Professor of Philosophy and Ethics at the University of San Francisco, he is editor and translator of the following works: *Towards a Transcendental Semiotics* (1994); *Ethics and the Theory of Rationality* (1996); and *The Underside of Modernity* (1996). He also is coeditor of *Liberation Theologies, Postmodernity and the Americas* (1997); *Latin America and Postmodernity: A Reader* (1997); and *Global Ethics* (1998). Mendieta publishes in an array of academic journals, including *Philosophy and Social Criticism*, *Praxis International*, *The Latino Review of Books*, and *The Journal of Hispanic/Latino Theology*.

In 1997 Mendieta organized a major national conference on Hispanics in the United States, entitled "Hispanics: Cultural Locations," at the University of San Francisco.

Ronald Takaki   A professor of Asian American Studies at the University of California, Berkeley, Takaki has had an enormous influence on the study of a multicultural America. His books are ubiquitous in university classes, particularly *From a Different Shore* (1987), *Strangers from a Different Shore* (1989), *Iron Cages: Race and Culture in 19th Century America* (1990), and *A Different Mirror: A History of Multicultural America* (1993).

In 1995 Takaki ignited a national controversy with the release of his book *Hiroshima: Why America Dropped the Bomb*. The tempest took Takaki on the major media circuit, including appearances on "Good Morning America," the "Today" show, and "Talk of the Nation."

Cornel West   Professor of Afro-American Studies and of the Philosophy of Religion at Harvard University, West is a nationally renowned commentator on the complexities of race relations in America.

West has authored *Race Matters* (1992), *Keeping Faith* (Routledge, 1993), and *The Future of the Race* (1996). His *Beyond Eurocentrism and Multiculturalism* (1993) won the National Book of the Year Award in 1994. His *American Evasion of Philosophy* (1989) is considered to be one of the most innovative re-readings of the American philosophical canon. He is also coeditor of the five-volume *Encyclopedia of African-American Culture and History* (1996).

Index of Names

★　　★　　★